Living in a Continual State of

Expectancy

To Uncle Verdell,
Read, Recieve &
Be Blessed!
I love You.
Your Niece,
Michelle

Living in a Continual State of

Expectancy

Michelle D. Houston

ALPHA-OMEGA PUBLISHING
MEMPHIS, TN 38141

First Printing 2002

Living in a Continual State of Expectancy
ISBN 0-9719385-0-4

Dedication

This book is lovingly dedicated to my family who is my first ministry. To Gerre Houston, my husband of 16 years – Thank you for being the godly man that you are. I love, appreciate and admire you exceedingly. You are indeed my soul mate, my prayer warrior and my closest friend. Thank you for all your support in encouraging and helping me to complete another assignment and dream.

♥ To my son Isaac, who is my first born, my miracle child, my little scientist and the one who keeps us laughing – Thank you son for your genuine, heartfelt love and affection. It helps me through each day. You are truly a child of destiny. Never give up on your dreams. Pursue God with all your heart, and all your ways will be established.

♥ To my daughter Mikaela, who is 'Momma's girl', my little artist and my miracle child as well – I love your unique sense of humor. You remind me so much of myself. Live your life to the fullest, reminding God of Himself.

Thank you guys so much for your patience in all the times you unselfishly "loaned" me out. I love you so very much.

Table of Contents

Acknowledgments

♥ To my Heavenly Father, Who has shown Himself strong in my life and with Whom I co-authored this book – I give You all the glory, honor and praise that's due to You. It is because of You that I live, I move and have my being.

♥ To my parents Dr. Jewell and Helen Bell – Thank you for all your encouragement and support. I appreciate and love you two so very much. You know, you might not have done everything right, but who has? I am highly favored and blessed by God to have you as my parents and I'm honored to be your daughter ☺ .

♥ To my Pastors Fred and Valerie Bennett – Thank you for laboring in the Word of God. Your labor is not in vain. The Word that you preach is being sealed in the hearts of many believers, bringing forth fruit in their lives, especially mine. I will never forget a message you preached, "Identifying Your Strengths". It was out of that message God spoke to my heart to write this book. Thank you.

♥ To my long time friend Shirley Akins – Thank you for being there through it all. Thank you for being a part of praying me into the family of God! Twenty-one years of knowing each other…WOW! I thank God for allowing our paths to meet and I'm grateful for the special friendship we share. You are definitely a pearl of great value. Thank you for all the encouragement and the hours you spent editing this work.

♥ To my dear friend Pam Pettis – Thank you for always believing the best of me. Your love as a sister, faithfulness as a friend, and richness as a prayer partner, is very precious to me. You are indeed another pearl of great value. I want to thank you as well, for all the encouragement and the hours you spent editing this work. For you to encourage me to write the next book as well as your eagerness to help with that one too, blesses me to no end. Girl, you are a jewel!

♥ To Felicia Johnson (Editor) and Terri Mitchell (Back cover photo) – Thank you for your time and contribution in making this book possible.

♥ To Stephanie Rooks who helped me to design the cover for this book – Thank you so much. You have helped eliminate a lot of frustration. I've learned a lot from you during the time we have worked together. You have really been a blessing. I thank God for you and your gift of creativity.

PREFACE

Dear Reader,

It gives me great joy to be able to share with you something that has changed my life. In order to experience a life of extraordinary favor with God, I believe God wants us to live in a continual state of expectancy. Many times we say that we are standing in faith for something, or we believe that God will do a certain thing, but the truth is often we are not operating in faith, because what we say we are in faith for, we don't really expect to happen. We're just hoping. It is not the kind of hope or expectation that is from God, but a hope that is defined as wishful thinking. It is a hope without the substance 'faith' (faith without expectation) and because of that, there is no manifestation. This is a place where many of God's people are.

God began to deal with me in this area of my life. As I sought the Lord, studied and applied the Word to my own life, I began to embrace the change that was taking place in me.

It is my prayer that the information contained in this book will challenge you to elevate your thinking and encourage you to live in a continual state of expectancy. I pray that you will be so stirred in your spirit, until you find yourself energized, renewed, changed by the power of God, and ushered into another level in Him.

To him who has an ear let him hear…

In His Righteousness,

Michelle Houston

1

FAITH AND HOPE

LINKED TO EXPECTATION

Now faith is the substance of things hoped for, the evidence of things not seen (Hebrews 11:1)

The word **faith** comes from the Greek word pistis (pis'-tis), which means persuasion; belief; to rely by inward certainty; agree, assure, have confidence, trust, yield.[1] The word **hope** comes from the Greek word elpis (el-pece'), which means to anticipate, usually with pleasure; a longing for, which is desire; expectation.[2] You can read Hebrews 11:1 this way – 'Now believing and relying on that inward certainty is the substance and foundation of things you are anticipating or expecting and the evidence or the proof of things not seen'. Faith is giving substance to things hoped for or desired and what is not yet manifested to the physical senses, but expected. Faith is the substance that God used to frame the world, and that same faith was transported by His words, so that the things which are seen were not made of things which are visible (Heb.11:3).

When God said in the book of Genesis, "Let there be light," the thought and desire were there first before He spoke it into existence. After He spoke it, He expected to see the manifestation of it, and He did (Gen. 1:3,4). He never spoke what was, but He only spoke what He desired and expected to see.

Expectation means to look forward to; it means to wait on; anticipation. Sometimes when we see the word "hope" in the Bible, it is referring to expectation. Expectation applies a considerable degree of confidence that a particular event will happen.[1] For example, when your friend calls you on the phone and tells you that he or she will be at your house to pick you up at three o'clock, you expect your friend to be there at that appointed time. Even during your preparation, you were expecting to hear the horn, the sound of the car in your driveway or a knock at the door. You may have even looked out of the window from time to time, awaiting his or her arrival. Expectation involves a change of vision because you are now looking for something. It also involves preparation and a change of position. You start preparing for something by positioning yourself to receive. A good example of this would be a woman who is pregnant. We say that she is expecting. She begins to prepare for the arrival of her baby by decorating, buying furniture, clothes, and other things she and the baby

14

would need. She is preparing and positioning herself to receive what she is expecting – a baby.

Faith is the substance – it is a literal unseen material. Hope is desire accompanied by expectation. To have one without the other is like having a car without wheels. You can't go anywhere without the wheels! The car and the wheels are equally important. Faith and hope are closely linked to expectation. Where there is faith and hope, there is expectation, and where there is expectation, there will be manifestation.

The Power of Expectation

In the summer of 1999, the air-conditioner stopped working in my car and I was miserable for about a week. My husband suggested that I take it to be repaired. Although I did not like the idea of taking it to an auto repair shop myself, I knew and understood his work schedule. I complained to him that when a woman takes her car somewhere to have it repaired, the mechanics usually give an outrageous diagnosis for a simple problem. Most women believe these mechanics and agree to pay the phenomenal fee to repair their car. After explaining to my husband what I thought about mechanics, I was convinced that if I took my car to have it repaired, I would be taken advantage of. In spite of what I thought, I convinced myself to have the air-conditioner repaired.

I walked into an auto repair shop, and I told them what the problem was. The mechanic on duty told me that it only needed a little freon. After putting freon in it and charging me $140, he also handed me an estimate of $1400 to repair it correctly, because it was leaking in several places. I was told the car needed a new air-conditioning system. I was angry and disappointed because he told me this after I paid $140. If the entire diagnosis were given before he put the freon in the car, I would have taken it somewhere else for a second opinion or estimate. At that point, I realized I had been deceived and threw away $140!

When I returned home, I sat at my kitchen table pondering what to do. I could not wait until my husband called so that I could express my anger. When I finally spoke to Gerre, he could tell by the tone of my voice that I was disappointed and angry. I told him all that happened at the repair shop and why I was angry. He seemed to be disappointed as well, but not angry. After hanging up the phone with him, the Lord asked me, "Why are you so angry?" I couldn't wait to answer Him, because I knew the Lord would see the injustice. I knew He would listen and understand my anger. I answered, "Lord, I just got ripped off and I'm angry about it. They knew before putting the freon in my car, that I needed a new air-conditioning system. The car was cool for a short time before it started blowing hot air again and I still had to pay $140!" I then became more angry because I thought if Gerre had taken the car to the mechanic, we would not have been out of $140. I began to find fault with everyone.

After expressing my anger and frustration to the Lord, He gently said to me, "You shouldn't be angry. You got just what you believed, spoke and expected. So, why are you angry?" After I fell under the conviction of the Holy Ghost, at that moment I realized my first mistake. I did not inquire of the Lord and trust His leading as to where to take my car. The Bible says in Proverbs 3:6, **"In all your ways acknowledge Him, and He shall direct your paths."** My second mistake was my mouth. In the Word of God, Jesus says in **Luke 6:45** (the latter part of the verse) **"for out of the abundance of the heart his mouth speaks."** I spoke what was in my heart, and what I expected came to pass. I stood up from my kitchen table and with a repentant heart, I began to pace the floor. I was no longer angry. Suddenly, I was quickened in my spirit to listen. I knew the Lord was about to reveal something to me, and He did. He led me to read the story of Elijah and the widow woman.

1 Kings 17:8-16

Then the word of the LORD came to him (Elijah), saying, [9]"Arise, go to Zarephath, which belongs to Sidon, and dwell there. See, I have commanded a widow there to provide for you." [10]So he arose and went to Zarephath. And when he came to the gate of the city, indeed a widow was there gathering sticks. And he called to her and said, "Please bring me a little water in a cup, that I may drink." [11]And as she was going to get it, he called to her and said, "Please bring me a morsel of bread in your hand." [12]So she said, "As the LORD your God lives, I do not have bread, only a handful of flour in a bin, and a little oil in a jar; and see, I am gathering a couple of sticks that I may go in and prepare it for myself and my son, that we may eat it, and die."[13]And Elijah said to her, "Do not fear; go and do as you have said, but make me a small cake from it first, and bring it to me; and afterward make some for yourself and your son. [14]For thus says the LORD God of Israel: "The bin of flour shall not be used up, nor shall the jar of oil run dry, until the day the LORD sends rain on the earth." [15]So she went away and did according to the word of Elijah; and she and he and her household ate for many days. [16]The bin of flour was not used up, nor did the jar of oil run dry, according to the word of the LORD which He spoke by Elijah.

This widow woman expected to cook her last meal, eat and then die. But God, Who is rich in mercy, saved her by giving her a word of hope and an opportunity to respond. Anytime you receive a word from God, there will always be an opportunity to respond. You will either respond in faith or you will respond in fear. She of course, responded in faith. God sent her the Word (faith comes by hearing, and hearing by the Word of God – Romans 10:17) to activate her faith, because faith brings expectation and expectation produces manifestation. The widow gave with the expectancy to receive (verse 15). God sent Elijah to the widow for her deliverance, not his. When she gave with the expectancy to receive what God had promised, she set in motion her own miracle. You can rest assured that expectation is a breeding ground for miracles. Her faith and expectation brought forth the manifestation of the promise. If she had not done what was expected of her, she would not have received the manifestation of what was promised. She went from not having enough to having more than enough. I saw the lesson to be learned from the incident with my car. My faith and expectation brought forth the manifestation of what I believed to be true. The Lord taught me that the same principle applies to my expectancy in Him. The Word of God says in the book of **James 1:5-8:**

"If any of you lacks wisdom, let him ask of God, who gives to

19

all liberally and without reproach, and it will be given to him. [6]But let him ask in faith, with no doubting, for he who doubts is like a wave of the sea driven and tossed by the wind. [7]For let not that man suppose that he will receive anything from the Lord; [8]he is a double-minded man, unstable in all his ways."

This passage of Scripture is speaking of wisdom, but it still applies to anything that you may ask of God. The key is to ask in faith with the expectancy to receive. By faith, receive it at the time you've asked for it, and then start looking (expecting) for the manifestation of it. Start rejoicing and thanking God for it as if you have it in your possession. If you are not expecting anything, then you will not receive anything. God is not moved by our needs or even by our desires. Our faith and expectation in Him are what moves Him. In other words, James is saying, the one who is not expecting what he asked for, let not that man expect or think that he will receive anything from the Lord. He is double-minded, asking but not expecting anything, which will cause him to be unstable in all his ways. James also calls this "doubting". For the one who doubts is like a wave of the sea driven and tossed by the wind. If you're tossed back and forth by circumstances, then you are unstable. To be unstable is to be unsettled, and to be stable is to be settled. It is hard to be tossed around when you are anchored and settled in God. You may ask, "What does it mean to be anchored in God?" It is when the Word of God becomes first place and the final authority in your life, regardless of circumstances.

The Importance of Renewing Your Mind

Do not be conformed to this world (this age), [fashioned after and adapted to its external, superficial customs], but be transformed (changed) by the [entire] renewal of your mind [by its new ideals and its new attitude], so that you may prove [for yourselves] what is the good and acceptable and perfect will of God, even the thing which is good and acceptable and perfect [in His sight for you]. (Romans 12:2 AMP)

Giving the Word of God first place and the final authority in your life can only be accomplished by knowing what the Word says. This comes by spending time in the Word of God, allowing your mind to be renewed by it and your life changed by it. God wants us to change the way we think. We have to reprogram our minds from the world's way of thinking to His way of thinking, which is found in the Word of God. We have been taught the world's way of doing things, and since we have been

21

transferred out of darkness (the world's system) into His marvelous light (kingdom living), we have to renew our minds. Our spirit has been made alive to Christ, but our minds must be renewed.

Romans 8:5-8 says, **"For those who live according to the flesh set their minds on the things of the flesh, but those *who live* according to the Spirit, the things of the Spirit. [6]For to be carnally minded *is* death, but to be spiritually minded *is* life and peace. [7]Because the carnal mind *is* enmity against God; for it is not subject to the law of God, nor indeed can be. [8]So then, those who are in the flesh cannot please God."**

The word enmity comes from the Greek word 'echthra' (ekh'-thrah), which means hateful; hostility; by implication a reason for opposition.[2] The Word of God is our instructional manual, teaching us how to live this abundant life that He has so freely given to us. To live a life pleasing to God, we must have the right kind of foundation – a firm foundation. We are to renew our minds on a day to day basis with the Word of God, and to be doers of the Word and not hearers only (James 1:22). In doing this, we are laying a firm foundation in which we are to build our lives upon. In **Luke 6:46-49 (NIV)**, Jesus talks about laying the right kind of foundation:

"Why do you call me, 'Lord, Lord,' and do not do what I

say? [47]I will show you what he is like who comes to me and hears my words and puts them into practice.[48]He is like a man building a house, who dug down deep and laid the foundation on rock. When a flood came, the torrent struck that house but could not shake it, because it was well built. [49]But the one who hears my words and does not put them into practice is like a man who built a house on the ground without a foundation. The moment the torrent struck that house, it collapsed and its destruction was complete."

Notice both men heard the Word, but only one was obedient to what Jesus said. When the storm came, one was left standing, unshaken, but the other collapsed, and its destruction was complete. What made one fall and the other stand? The difference between the two was the foundation. The house that stood against the storm was built on a solid foundation. If we are doers of the Word, the foundation that our lives are built upon will be solid, and when the storms come against us, we will be unmovable, firmly rooted in the Word of God.

There is life in the Word of God, and we are to live as if it's our very lives – and it is! In **Luke 4:4** Jesus said, **"It is written, 'Man shall not live and be sustained by (on) bread alone, but by every word and expression of God'"** (AMP).

So many of the problems we face are rooted in our thinking patterns. Wrong thinking is a breeding ground for wrong actions. All battles begin in the mind, therefore, it is necessary that we align our thoughts with God thoughts. This is a process that will take time and study. As we spend time in the Word of God, change is taking place in our minds and because of that, our very lives will begin to change. Let's look at **2 Corinthians 10: 4, 5:**

For the weapons of our warfare *are* not carnal but mighty in God for pulling down strongholds, [5]casting down arguments and every high thing that exalts itself against the knowledge of God, bringing every thought into captivity to the obedience of Christ.

Satan always tries to set up strongholds in our minds. It's a place where we are held in bondage due to wrong thinking and a place where certain views and attitudes are concentrated or meditated upon. Verse 5 tells us where those strongholds are. The war that wages against us is in our minds, which is the battleground. There is never a war without weapons. If we are going to battle evil spirits and influences, we need spiritual weapons. We would look silly going to war without weapons. God has given us weapons to conquer every battle. One of those weapons is the Word of God. **Ephesians 6:10-18** says:

"Finally, my brethren, be strong in the Lord and in the power of His might. [11]Put on the whole armor of God, that

you may be able to stand against the wiles of the devil. [12]For we do not wrestle against flesh and blood, but against principalities, against powers, against the rulers of the darkness of this age, against spiritual *hosts* of wickedness in the heavenly *places.* [13]Therefore take up the whole armor of God, that you may be able to withstand in the evil day, and having done all, to stand. [14]Stand therefore, having girded your waist with truth, having put on the breastplate of righteousness, [15]and having shod your feet with the preparation of the gospel of peace; [16]above all, taking the shield of faith with which you will be able to quench all the fiery darts of the wicked one. [17]And take the helmet of salvation, <u>and the sword of the Spirit, which is the Word of God;</u> [18]praying always with all prayer and supplication in the Spirit, being watchful…"

That's why it is so important to spend time in the Word, meditating on the Word, doing the Word, speaking the Word and praying the Word because by it, we overcome, we conquer and we win. Praise God!

Other weapons we have are prayer and praise. Our prayer and praise should be full of the Word, but it is not prayer nor praise if it is not from the heart. Both prayer and praise must be genuine. When the three are involved (the Word, prayer and praise), you are creating a dangerous atmosphere for the enemy, and he hates it. You are also creating an atmosphere for God's presence to dwell, and He loves it. There is nothing more paralyzing to the enemy than for us to give God praise in the midst of a storm. However, we do not have to wait until we are in a storm to praise Him. Praise should forever be upon our lips.

God has given us everything we need to live a victorious life. He did not leave us helpless, but He placed The Holy Ghost, Who is our Helper, on the inside of us. We have the ability to tear down strongholds that we have allowed the enemy to build in our minds. Many times he is able to do this because we are not careful in what we hear and how we hear. If what we are hearing is not lining up with the Word of God, then we need to take that thought captive to the obedience of Christ. We have the ability to control our thoughts. Many times we fail to deal with our carnal thoughts because we know that no one else knows what we are thinking. We cannot overcome wrong thinking by thinking good thoughts, but we overcome wrong thoughts by speaking faith-filled words. If we do not control our thoughts, our thoughts will control us, and consequently, our actions will follow.

The mind of God, the heart of God and the will of God are found in the Word of God. Once the Word is on the inside of us, which comes as a result of our meditating, speaking, and applying the Word to our lives, it is then that our very lives will display the life of God. We will go from reading the Word to doing the Word and from doing the Word to being the Word. We will be changed from glory to glory! Why? Because **our inward man is being renewed day by day (2 Cor. 4:16).** As we are renewing our minds, we are also learning other valuable lessons. These include knowing who we are in Him, Who He is in us and the rich heritage that is ours, because of the covenant we have with Him. In 2 Timothy, Paul tells us what God has given us, and what He has not given us. Let's take a look at it:

2 Timothy 1:7 (AMP)

For God did not give us a spirit of timidity (of cowardice, of craven and cringing and fawning fear), but [He has given us a spirit] of power and of love and of calm and well-balanced mind and discipline and self-control.

Fear does not come from God, because fear brings torment. Fear is perverted faith. It produces negative results, just the same as faith produces God-kind of results. Fear gives the devil access in our lives to devour us whereas faith gives God access in our lives to carry out His will and to meet the needs of His people. Fear keeps us in bondage whereas walking by faith keeps us free. **Romans 8:15** says, **"For you did not receive the spirit of bondage again to fear, but you received the Spirit of adoption by**

whom we cry out, 'Abba, Father'." It is the same Spirit that is of miraculous power, ability, strength, abundance, might, love and that of a discipline, self-control, <u>sober and sound mind.</u> **Now we have received, not the spirit of the world, but the Spirit who is from God, that we may know the things that have been freely given to us by God (1 Cor. 2:12).** We have to receive what God has given us by faith and operate in it. However, we are to reject and attack the spirit of fear, because it will produce results that we do not desire.

Philippians 2:1-5

Therefore if *there is* any consolation in Christ, if any comfort of love, if any fellowship of the Spirit, if any affection and mercy, [2]fulfill my joy by being like-minded, having the same love, *being* of one accord, of one mind. [3]<u>Let</u> nothing *be done* through selfish ambition or conceit, but in lowliness of mind <u>let</u> each esteem others better than himself. [4]<u>Let</u> each of you look out not only for his own interests, but also for the interests of others. [5]<u>Let</u> this mind be in you which was also in Christ Jesus...

As Christians, you and I have been given a new nature, which is actually the nature of God deposited on the inside of us when we were born again. Paul admonishes us to LET this mind be in us which was also in Christ Jesus and we can, because we have been given the ability to. We have

28

the mind of Christ! You may say, "We don't really have the mind of Christ because He was perfect and we're not." The Bible says, "...as He is, so are we in this world" (1 John 4:17). The Bible also says that we have the mind of Christ and a new heart and spirit. Whether we feel like we do or not is irrelevant. If He said we have it, then we do. God cannot lie. We are to believe what God says about us, rather than what we see or feel. We cannot walk with God, unless we agree with God. He made us, therefore, He knows us and He knows what He put in us.

Ezekiel 36:26,27

I will give you a new heart and put a new spirit within you; I will take the heart of stone out of your flesh and give you a heart of flesh. [27]I will put My Spirit within you and cause you to walk in My statutes, and you will keep My judgments and do them.

1 Corinthians 2:14-16

But the natural man does not receive the things of the Spirit of God, for they are foolishness to him; nor can he know _them,_ because they are spiritually discerned. [15]But he who is spiritual judges all things, yet he himself is _rightly_ judged by no one. [16]For _"who has known the mind of the LORD that he may instruct Him?"_ But we have the mind of Christ.

1 Peter 1:13 NIV

Therefore, prepare your minds for action; be self-controlled (sober, possessing a sound mind); set your hope (expectation) fully on the grace to be given you when Jesus Christ is revealed.

We are to no longer be conformed to this world and its way of thinking and doing things. We are to be transformed (changed) by the entire renewal of our minds, having new ideas and a new attitude, so that we may prove what is that good and acceptable and perfect will of God (Romans 12:2).

Therefore do not be unwise, but understand what the will of the Lord *is* (Ephesians 5:17).

2

LIVING UNASHAMED

Uphold me according to Your word, that I may live; And do not let me be ashamed of my hope (Psalms 119:116)

It is not the heart of God for His people to live in shame or to be made ashamed. In the above Scripture, the word **ashamed** is the Hebrew word 'bush' (boosh), which means to be disappointed or delayed.[1] The word **hope** is translated in the Hebrew 'seber' (say-ber) as expectation.[2] You can read this Scripture this way – 'Uphold me according to Your Word, that I may live; and do not let me be disappointed or delayed because of my expectation'.

There have been times in my own life when I would secretly trust God (at least I thought I was trusting God). I would not share with people what I was believing God for, especially if it was material things. I feared what people would say or think if it did not come to pass. I thought that I would be made ashamed and looked upon as having a lot of zeal, but no faith. Many of God's people are experiencing the same fear. We have a promise from God in **Romans 10:11, "...No man who believes in Him [who adheres to, relies on, and trusts in Him] will [ever] be put to shame or be disappointed" (AMP).** God is faithful to His Word. He longs for us to trust Him. He does not want us to be ashamed of our expectation. David said in **Psalm 62:5, "My soul wait, silently for God alone, for my expectation** (the thing that I long for and expect)[3] *is* **from Him."** Our expectation is from God. When we are believing God for something, He wants us to expect Him to do it. We are to trust Him, rest in Him and wait on Him, with the expectancy that what He has promised, He will bring to pass. Just as David said in **Psalm 37:3,4, "Trust in the Lord, and do good; dwell in the land, and feed on His faithfulness. [4]Delight yourself also in the LORD, And He shall give you the desires of your heart."**

If we do our part, we can expect God to do His part. We should never feel ashamed when we are standing and believing God for something that we do not yet have in our possession. If we are feeling ashamed of our expectation, it is not because God is making us feel that way. It is because we have listened to the lie of the enemy, and we have begun to meditate on that lie until it brought shame into our lives. He whispers lies like, "See, you have told all those people that you were believing God for a house, and it has been three years now. So, where's that house that you believed God for? People now think you are crazy and they are not going to believe anything else you say. You might as well quit telling others what you expect from God. Come on now, you have to be realistic. If God was going to do it, He would have done it by now."

All of a sudden we begin to meditate on what seems to be true, and then we are covered with shame. We were pregnant with expectancy, but what we do next is try to hide our pregnancy. Then we even sometimes agree with the devil when we say, "I am not going to say anything else to people about what I'm believing God for, because if it does not happen, I will not be made ashamed." The devil then knows that his lie has worked. This does not mean that you have to go around telling people everything you are believing God for. Many times, we wait until we have received something, and then we say to others, "God did it." We then go into details describing how God did it for us. We do this many times to avoid being made ashamed, 'just in case God doesn't come through.' People need to hear our faith speak. We need to hear ourselves speak what we believe in faith. Faith comes by hearing, and hearing by the Word of God. Faith is not for what we can see in the natural, but for what we don't see in the natural.

My husband and I were married for three years and living in an apartment before we bought our first house. Most of our friends already had houses before we bought ours. At that time, we really desired to have our own house, but in the natural, there was no way possible that we could see buying one. We did not have the money for a down payment. Gerre had been laid off. I had just started a new job, the bills were piling up and the pressure was on. I was beginning to feel ashamed of our circumstances. I would not invite friends over, because I was ashamed that we were living in a small apartment and they had houses. Most of our friends had two cars and we only had one! I had begun to compare where we were to where I thought they were.

After praying and seeking the Lord concerning our needs and a desire for a home, God began to deal with me about my attitude towards our friends, which was a result of wrong thinking. He also dealt with me about being envious of what they had, and ashamed of what we did not have. After getting my heart and attitude right, God taught me an important lesson in why it is not wise to compare yourselves among yourselves. Comparing takes your eyes off of the Lord and on people. It will cause you to begin to trust in your own abilities in changing your circumstances, rather than trusting in the Lord and His ability. It will cause you to strive to keep up with people rather than striving to please the Lord. It all stems from pride. A person's pride will bring him low, but a person that walks humbly and upright before the Lord, in due time, God will exalt him.

Before long, I was no longer comparing us and what we had to our friends and what they had, but I was rejoicing in how the Lord was blessing them. We could not see in the natural how God was going to bless us, but we were confident that He would. We believed the Word of God and what we believed, we had begun to speak. In spite of our circumstances, we expected God to bless and honor our requests. We had God's Word on it:

Philippians 4:6

Be anxious for nothing, but in everything by prayer and supplication, with thanksgiving, let your requests be made known to God.

We began to rejoice in our expectation, rather than being ashamed of our expectation. I began to encourage Gerre instead of complaining to him. We worked our way out of being ashamed by rejoicing, being thankful, and trusting the Lord to meet our needs and to grant us our hearts' desire. It wasn't long before the Lord granted our request. He even went beyond what we requested of Him. Gerre was blessed with a new job making four times as much as he had made before. God placed it on someone's heart to bless us with a large down payment for a house. He gave us favor during the whole process in buying a house. He also blessed us with a second vehicle!

No matter what the circumstances are, we can be confident in knowing that God does not want us worrying and fretting over it, but trusting Him. If you worry, you will speak fear-filled words, but if you are trusting in the Lord, you will speak faith-filled words. Whatever you believe, that's what you will speak. ...**For out of the abundance of the heart, the mouth speaks (Matthew 12:34).** Look at Paul's circumstances in the book of Philippians. He was thrown in prison and awaiting trial. He saw his trial as an opportunity to witness for Christ. He encourages the Philippians to remain steadfast in the face of opposition. Whatever position or situation Paul was in, he lived his life unashamed. Look at what he said to the church at Philippi:

Philippians 1:12-20

"But I want you to know, brethren, that the things *which happened* to me have actually turned out for the furtherance of the gospel, [13]so that it has become evident to the whole palace guard, and to all the rest, that my chains are in Christ; [14]and most of the brethren in the Lord, having become confident by my chains, are much more bold to speak the word without fear. [15]Some indeed preach Christ even from envy and strife, and some also from goodwill: [16]The former preach Christ from selfish ambition, not sincerely, supposing to add affliction to my chains; [17]but the latter out of love, knowing that I am appointed for the defense of the gospel. [18]What then? Only *that* in every way,

whether in pretense or in truth, Christ is preached; and in this I rejoice, yes, and will rejoice. [19]For I know that this will turn out for my deliverance through your prayer and the supply of the Spirit of Jesus Christ, [20]according to my earnest expectation and hope that in nothing I shall be ashamed, but with all boldness, as always, so now also Christ will be magnified in my body, whether by life or by death."

Paul was confident that his situation was going to turn out to his advantage, for his good and for his deliverance. He said it was according to his earnest expectation and hope, that in nothing he should be made ashamed. This is a man who refused to be made ashamed, no matter what the circumstances were. He often admonished and reminded Timothy of his responsibilities towards the work of the ministry. One of the first things that Paul told Timothy in his second letter to him was to not be ashamed of the testimony of the Lord.

2 Timothy 1:6-8,12

Therefore I remind you to stir up the gift of God which is in you through the laying on of my hands. [7]For God has not given us a spirit of fear, but of power and of love and of a sound mind. [8]Therefore do not be ashamed of the testimony of our Lord, nor of me His prisoner, but share with me in the sufferings for the gospel according to the power of God...

[12]**For this reason I also suffer these things; <u>nevertheless I am not ashamed</u>, for I know whom I have believed and am persuaded that He is able to keep what I have committed to Him until that Day.**

It was obvious that Paul was not ashamed of the testimony of the Lord Jesus Christ, if he admonished Timothy not to be. His life, according to the Scriptures, reflected that as well. In Romans 1:16, he declared, **"I am not ashamed of the gospel of Christ, for it is the power of God to salvation for everyone who believes, for the Jew first and also for the Greek."**

God wants us to live our lives unashamed. It is His will for us, just as it was with Paul, that we should not be made ashamed. Never be ashamed of where you are nor of your circumstances, because your circumstances are subject to change. Many times we are also made ashamed by comparing another man's success to our own success. We make the mistake of judging success by what a person has or does not have, and by his or her appearance. Real success is not based on those things. It is living a life obedient to the Lord and accomplishing every thing that God assigns us to do. It is living unashamed, totally relying and trusting in the Lord, and exercising your God-given potential in fulfilling your purpose. Now, that's success!

The prophet Joel spoke of a time coming where the

people of God would never be put to shame, because of the Lord refreshing and restoring His people. I believe we are living in that time.

Joel 2:25-27

[25] **"So I will restore to you the years that the swarming locust has eaten,**
   The crawling locust,
   The consuming locust,
   And the chewing locust,
   My great army which I sent among you.
[26] **You shall eat in plenty and be satisfied,**
   And praise the name of the LORD your God,
   Who has dealt wondrously with you;
   And My people shall never be put to shame.
[27] **Then you shall know that I** *am* **in the midst of Israel:**
   I *am* **the LORD your God**
   And there is no other.
   My people shall never be put to shame.

Psalm 40:4a says, "Blessed *is* the man who makes the LORD his trust." Why? Because according to **Romans 10:11, "The Scripture says, 'no man who believes in Him [who adheres to, relies on, and trusts in Him] will [ever] be put to shame or be disappointed'" (AMP)**...and because of that, that man is blessed!

Nothing Happens — Until You Say It

The Word of God says in **Amos 3:3, "Can two walk together, unless they are agreed?"** If we are going to walk with God, we have to agree with God and trust and know that His way is best for us. We have to believe what He says about us despite what we see in the natural. We have to make sure we are speaking the right things. In order to do that, we have to change the way we think, and by changing the way we think, we will speak differently. God has given us the choice of life or death, and He says that the power of the two rest in our tongue. Consider these two passages of Scriptures:

Proverbs 18:20-21

"A man's stomach shall be satisfied from the fruit of his mouth; *From* **the produce of his lips he shall be filled. ²¹Death and life** *are* **in the power of the tongue, and those who love it will eat its fruit."**

Matthew 12: 36-37

"But I say to you that for every idle word men may speak, they will give account of it in the day of judgment. ³⁷For by your words you will be justified, and by your words you will be condemned."

Your words are so important. God wants to get us to the point that we are saying the same things He is saying. This is why it is so important to study and meditate on the Word of God, and allow it to be first priority and final authority in our lives. When we spend time in the Word, it gives God something to work with. He is working the Word on the inside of us so that it will produce change in every area of our lives. The Word of God also trains us to learn the voice of God. If you believe the written Word, you will find it much easier to follow the inward witness of the voice of the Spirit. When He speaks, you will know it is Him because what you are hearing is right in line with His written Word. The Amplified Bible says in **Hebrews 4:12a** that the Word of God **"is alive and full of power making it active, operative, energizing, and effective."** It is alive and full of power, active and operative on the inside of us! What is on the inside of us will be evident to others by what we say. The Word is received by faith. It is deposited in our hearts, and the Holy Ghost brings it to our remembrance (our mind) and out of the abundance of the heart, the mouth speaks. Then His words become our words. **Isaiah 55:10-11 (TLB)** says: **"As the rain and snow come down from heaven and stay upon the ground to water the earth, and cause the grain to grow and to produce seed for the farmer and bread for the hungry, so also is My word. I send it out, and it always produces fruit. It shall accomplish all I want it to and prosper everywhere I send it."**

Now, how is God going to send forth His Word? Through His representatives on the earth. We are God's representatives! That's why we have to give voice to the Word of God. His Word will not return void. There is power in the spoken Word, but in order for that power to operate in our lives or circumstances, we have to give voice to it. Every time we speak the Word of God in any given situation, the Word is activated. For example, if there is no peace in your home, then activate peace by speaking it. Walk in it by faith, believing that peace is now being activated and created in your home. Then, allow that peace to lead you. Before you know it, the atmosphere of your home has changed. When you speak things, expect it to happen. Nothing happens, until you say it! The Word says, **"Let the weak say, "I am strong""** **(Joel 3:10).** If you continue to say, "I am strong," then strength will manifest in your body through your confession. If you are tired and have no strength, don't complain about it. Every time you say, "Oh, I am so tired" or "I am so tired of..." you are giving strength to what you are saying.

God responds not to your need, but to your faith and expectancy. He is listening for His Word to fulfil His Word. If you say it (faith comes by hearing), hearing yourself will activate your faith, and then He will show up to respond to your faith by way of hearing your words.

Never speak your circumstances (you'll give strength to it), but speak TO your circumstances.

I can remember when a miracle took place in our lives, because we would not let go of a promise we had from God, until we saw the manifestation of that promise. Before that happened, we faced many obstacles. I had begun to speak the circumstances, and Gerre was speaking the solution, which was the Word of God. We appeared to be in agreement with one another, but we were not speaking the same things. Here's what happened:

Gerre and I were married in September of 1986. We had planned to start a family a year later. A year later came and went. I had not conceived yet. I began to be concerned and wondered if something was wrong with him or myself. After going to the doctor, I was told everything was fine. Another year passed and nothing happened. In going back to the doctor to have some tests done, I was told that I had an 18% chance of getting pregnant. I was discouraged. An 18% chance of getting pregnant was like 0% chance to me. We began to look to God.

After another year, I gave up in believing God. I allowed doubt and unbelief to set in. I then came up with a solution, adoption. I would mention it to Gerre, but he was

43

not agreeing to it. Every time someone would ask, "When are you two going to start a family?" I would always say, "I don't know, I just can't seem to get pregnant. It doesn't look like I'm going to ever have a child." Little did I know, every time I spoke like that, I was giving strength to what I perceived to be a problem. What you don't know can hurt you. Thank God there is a solution for ignorance...KNOWLEDGE!

One day, the Lord told Gerre that I was going to conceive, and he was going to bless him with a son. He led him to a Scripture in Romans 9:9. This is how the Lord spoke to Gerre, **"For this is the word of promise: At this time I will come and Shelly** (my nickname) **shall have a son."** He later told me what the Lord spoke to him and shared the Scripture with me as well. I was not at all excited like he was. In fact, I was angry because I did not want to get my 'hopes' up, only to be disappointed again. I responded to Gerre with a "yea, right". I did not believe he had heard from God. I thought he was only trying to talk me out of wanting to adopt. Everyday he was thanking God for our son. There was such a joy in his heart and such a confidence in his voice about it. I was beginning to become resentful towards Gerre, because I was not joyful or confident like he was.

I was home alone one day and I began to cry out to

God. I did not like what I had become, bitter. The Lord began to deal with me. His goodness led me to repentance. After being in His presence, I had forgotten about wanting a child. I just wanted to bathe in His presence. I was broken before Him, but refreshed. The Lord then spoke to me. He assured me that He wanted to bless me with a son, but it would not happen until I got in agreement with my husband. He then said to me, "Nothing is impossible with Me and nothing is impossible to him who believes, however, nothing will happen until you say it." I then whispered the very words that Mary said when the angel told her that she would conceive. "...Let it be done to me according to Your word" (Luke 1:38).

I shared with Gerre what the Lord spoke to me during my quiet time with Him. We began to rejoice, pray and thank God for our son. My countenance, my heart and my confession had changed. We were joyfully walking in agreement. Approximately three months later, I was pregnant. We were even told by doctors that I would not be able to carry it, but that did not move us. We were already telling people that it was a boy. They would ask if we had an ultrasound, but we would answer them, "No". We were confident in what we heard and we were waiting expectantly. I later had an ultrasound at the request of my doctor. They confirmed the baby was a boy and that he appeared to be healthy. At the appointed time Isaac was born. He was the seed of promise. The promise to us was established when we both spoke it. During the pregnancy, there were some difficult times. Discouragement would knock at my door, but I had a promise from God, and I would not let go of that promise. I would run to that secret place, where I found shelter…in His presence. I would <u>say</u> **of the Lord, "*He is* my refuge and my fortress; My God, in Him I will trust" (Psalm 91:2).** Just to say Who He was, strengthened me. It still strengthens me today to worship Him and to acknowledge Him for Who He is.

When you recognize and acknowledge God for Who He is, there is something about you saying it. He becomes more real or personal to you, just the same as when you learn someone's name. By calling them by their name, you're becoming more personable to them. God knows and calls us by name (John 10:3), and He desires for us to know Him and call Him by His name. I encourage you to learn the many names of God. It will help you to know His character.

We say, "Jesus is Lord," and He is Lord, whether we say it or not, BUT, He's not Lord of 'YOUR' life until you acknowledge and confess Him as Lord. You have to say it! The truth is, you did not get saved because you knew Jesus died on the cross bearing your sins, was buried and rose again on the third day. You weren't saved because you believed it with all your heart, though it was part of the process, but it was not complete until you said it!

Romans 10:8-10

But what does it say? *"The word is near you, in your mouth and in your heart"* (that is, the word of faith, which we preach): <u>that if you confess (say) with your mouth</u> the Lord Jesus and believe in your heart that God has raised Him from the dead, you will be saved. For with the heart one believes unto righteousness, <u>and with the mouth confession is made unto salvation.</u>

If God had never said anything, the world would have never been. Before something was ever created, God said it first, and He expected it to be created when He spoke it. So you see, your words are very important. Angels are even dispatched to carry out the Word in our lives. They have been put here by God to serve us. They hearken to the voice of the Word. That is why we have to give voice to the Word of God. **Psalm 103:20** speaks of this:

"Bless the LORD, you His angels, who excel in strength, who do His word (His command), **heeding the voice of His word"** **(NRSV – His spoken word).**

This Scripture speaks of the angels excelling in strength. It is the voice of the spoken Word that gives them strength.

Every time you speak the Word of God (giving voice to it), angels are increasing in strength, and they are carrying out His commands. The Word of God says in **1 Peter 4:11a, "If anyone speaks, *let him speak* as the oracles of God."** In other words, let him speak as though God Himself were speaking through him. When you speak the Word of God, it is just as if God Himself spoke it. He has given us that authority. We are His representatives in the earth. Nothing will ever happen in the earth or in your circumstances, until you open your mouth and say it first. To obtain anything – healing, deliverance or prosperity, it is going to take more than knowledge and revelation. To get results or manifestation, you are going to have to say it. One of the greatest tools we will ever have is our mouth, and what we do with it is crucial. It is placed there on our faces for more than just to eat with, to display an expression, or to make us look better. We are to use our mouths to speak the very words of God. Angels stand in attention ready to carry out the Word of God that you speak. God gives them the order to carry out His Word, since He is the High Priest of our confession (Heb. 3:1). He hastens over His Word to perform it (Jer.1:12 KJV). The word 'hasten' comes from the Hebrew word 'shaw-kad', which means to be alert; sleepless; to be on the lookout; to watch for.[4] God is always alert and sleeplessly on the lookout watching and listening for His Word to be spoken in the earth, to perform it.

48

In the book of Daniel, chapter 9, Daniel intercedes for the people of Israel. He petitions God for forgiveness while reminding God of His righteousness, His mercy and His covenant. Look at verses 19-23:

"**O Lord, hear! O Lord, forgive! O Lord, listen and act! Do not delay for Your own sake, my God, for Your city and Your people are called by Your name.**" **[20]Now while I *was* speaking, praying, and confessing my sin and the sin of my people Israel, and presenting my supplication before the LORD my God for the holy mountain of my God, [21]yes, while I *was* speaking in prayer, the man Gabriel, whom I had seen in the vision at the beginning, being caused to fly swiftly, reached me about the time of the evening offering. [22]And he informed *me,* and talked with me, and said, "O Daniel, I have now come forth to give you skill to understand. [23]At the beginning of your supplications the command went out, and I have come to tell *you,* for you *are* greatly beloved; therefore consider the matter, and understand the vision:**

The angel Gabriel continues to give Daniel understanding of the vision he has, but notice in verse 23 what Daniel was asking God to do. The command was given to the angels to carry out Daniel's request. We're going to skip to chapter 10, starting at verse 10:

"**Suddenly, a hand touched me, which made me tremble on my knees and *on* the palms of my hands. [11]And he said to me,**

"O Daniel, man greatly beloved, understand the words that I speak to you, and stand upright, for I have now been sent to you." While he was speaking this word to me, I stood trembling. **[12]Then he said to me, "Do not fear, Daniel, for from the first day that you set your heart to understand, and to humble yourself before your God, <u>your words were heard; and I have come because of your words.</u>"** The Amplified Bible says in the latter part of this verse: **"I have come as a consequence of [and in response to] your words."**

The angel was sent to Daniel in response to his words. The angel heeded to the voice of the Word! Daniel put God in remembrance of His covenant...His Word. Now, if God is watching over His Word to perform it, do you know that the devil is watching over his word to perform it? That's why it is important to speak the right things and not speak anything contrary to the Word of God. The devil does not know whether his lie worked or not until you open your mouth. He knows where you are by what you say. Our mouths are a tool to be used as a creative force in the earth, speaking forth the Word of God. Jesus reinforces this message in **Mark 11:23 KJV:**

"For verily I say unto you, That whosoever shall say unto this mountain, Be thou removed, and be thou cast into the sea; and shall not doubt in his heart, but shall believe that those things which he saith shall come to pass; he shall have whatsoever he saith."

The word 'doubt' means to waver, hesitate or stagger.[5] Whatever you do not believe, you will not expect. It goes back to the meaning of the word 'expectation'. It means to look forward to; it applies a considerable degree of confidence that a particular event will happen.[6] Faith and expectation will eliminate doubt and unbelief. This Scripture could be paraphrased like this:

Whosoever shall say unto this mountain, be thou removed and be thou cast into the sea; and shall look forward to with confidence, believing that those things which he say shall come to pass; he shall have whatsoever he says.

I asked God once, "What does a mountain represent?" He answered, "Anything that tries to exalt itself above the knowledge of God...anything that tries to stand in the way of you fulfilling your purpose...anything that comes to hinder the Word from producing fruit in your life...any closed door that I did not close...any adversity, problem or circumstance that 'SEEMS' to be bigger than Me." After that answer, I came to the realization that I have the authority to move those mountains (obstacles or circumstances) that the enemy tries to set up in my life.

The words that we speak are powerful when they are spoken in faith. Make a quality decision that whatever you do not want in your life, speak to it to be gone and make the necessary changes that need to be made. Whatever you want in your life that is not there, speak it into existence, calling those things which do not exist as though they did (Romans 4:17). Receive it by faith and walk as though you already possess it.

If you don't desire it, then don't say it nor pray it! Start speaking what you desire into existence. There are so many promises of God that He's longing to fulfil in our lives, but we have to trust and expect Him to bring them to pass. **"For all the promises of God in Him *are* Yes, and in Him Amen, to the glory of God through us"** (2 Cor.1:20). When we are walking in obedience to the Word of God and putting God in remembrance of His Word, He cannot refuse us. Why? Because He cannot deny Himself. If He said it, He will fulfil it. The key to it is finding out what He said and what's been made available to us.

God not only cares about our needs, but also our very desires. He is a good God! In any circumstance or situation, He has given us the authority to speak the Word of God. There are only two real choices in life and it is summed up in **Deuteronomy 30:19, "I call heaven and earth as witnesses today against you, *that* I have set before you life and death, blessing and cursing; therefore choose life, that both you and your descendants may live."**

God is so good, He gives us choices and then tells us which one to choose. It is like a teacher who gives you a test, and then gives you the answers! You would be foolish to choose the wrong answer when he or she gave you the right answer. It is foolish for us to speak contrary to the Word of God. There is life in the Word, therefore choose life! If you choose life, then let your words be full of life.

"My son, if your heart is wise, My heart will rejoice—indeed, I myself; Yes, my inmost being will rejoice when your lips speak right things" (Proverbs 23:15, 16).

Your Confidence Rewarded

Faith comes by hearing the Word, but confidence comes by knowing the Word. I am not speaking of memorizing and quoting the Word, but KNOWING the Word. I'm speaking of being acquainted with the Word, getting to know the Word by spending time in the Word, gaining wisdom, understanding and revelation knowledge. It is becoming one with the Word. Because God and His Word are one, you cannot know one without the other. Therefore, the KNOWING I'm speaking of involves intimacy. Confidence comes by knowing or being intimate with the Word. **Proverbs 14:26 (AMP) says:**

"In the reverent and worshipful <u>fear of the Lord there is</u> <u>strong confidence,</u> and His children shall always have a place of refuge."

When you know the Word of God and you are confident, secure and established in it, you will not allow any room in your life for compromise. What you compromise to get, you will ultimately lose it. When you are secure in the Word of God and confident of who you are in Him and Who He is in you, you will not bow down to the pressures of the enemy. You will stand on the Word of God, being confident that the Word of God, which is the will of God, will manifest in your life and in your circumstances. With that kind of confidence in the Word, your circumstances will have to bow to the Word that you speak.

In the book of Daniel, chapter 3, a king by the name of Nebuchadnezzar, who was the king of Babylon, made a gold image and sent word to gather all the high officials, and the people together to come to the dedication of this image that he had set up. They assembled. He issued the command that at the time the people heard the sound of all kinds of music, they were to fall down and worship the gold image that he had set up. Whoever did not fall down and worship was to be cast immediately into the midst of a burning fiery furnace. There were three young Hebrew men who the king had set over the affairs of the province of Babylon. They were Hananiah, Mishael, and Azariah whom we know as Shadrach, Meshach, and Abed-Nego. They would neither serve pagan gods, nor worship the gold image that the king had set up. Look at what happened:

Daniel 3:13-18

Then Nebuchadnezzar, in rage and fury, gave the command to bring Shadrach, Meshach, and Abed-Nego. So they brought these men before the king. Nebuchadnezzar spoke, saying to them, "*Is it* true, Shadrach, Meshach, and Abed-Nego, *that* you do not serve my gods or worship the gold image which I have set up? Now if you are ready at the time you hear the sound of the horn, flute, harp, lyre, *and* psaltery, in symphony with all kinds of music, and you fall down and worship the image which I have made, *good!* But if you do not worship, you shall be cast immediately into the midst of a burning fiery furnace. And who *is* the god who will deliver you from my hands?"

(Notice how they answered Nebuchadnezzar)

Shadrach, Meshach, and Abed-Nego answered and said to the king, "O Nebuchadnezzar, we have no need to answer you in this matter. If that *is the case,* our God whom we serve is able to deliver us from the burning fiery furnace, and He will deliver *us* from your hand, O king. But if not, let it

be known to you, O king, that we do not serve your gods, nor will we worship the gold image which you have set up."

Despite their circumstances, they were not only filled with expectancy in their hearts that God would deliver them, but they spoke with confidence that God would deliver them. They were confident that God was not only able but also willing to deliver them. If you continue to read the story, you will find that God did not only deliver them, but He rewarded them as well. Shadrach, Meshach, and Abed-Nego did not kneel down to pray when they were confronted, so God didn't have a prayer to answer. He was listening to their conversation with the king. How they responded to the king is what caused God to respond to them. Their faith spoke, and God answered them in the form of their deliverance. They did not compromise, but was strong in what they believed. They trusted in their God, and they were not made ashamed. In the end, the king acknowledged their God as God, and he promoted them, but behind that promotion was God. God rewarded them because they refused to compromise and it pleased the Lord to deliver them because of their trust and confidence in Him. Miracles most often occur among people who are bold about God and who would dare to trust Him. There are times in our lives when we will be tempted to compromise, but if we do not bow to the pressure of the enemy, God will show up every time. It will please Him to deliver us.

God is looking for faith, and He is listening for our expectation, and our expectation should be based upon the Word of God. When our expectation is based on the Word of God, then we can walk with confidence knowing that what He has promised, He is able to perform. He is not only able, but He is willing. He expects us to expect Him to do what He says He will do! Abraham's faith was an example of how God wants our faith to be. Let's look at it:

Romans 4:17-25

[17] (as it is written, *"I have made you a father of many nations"*) in the presence of Him whom he believed—God, who gives life to the dead and calls those things which do not exist as though they did; [18]who, contrary to hope, in hope believed, so that he became the father of many nations, according to what was spoken, *"So shall your descendants be."* [19]And not being weak in faith, he did not consider his own body, already dead (since he was about a hundred years old), and the deadness of Sarah's womb. [20]He did not waver at the promise of God through unbelief, but was strengthened in faith, giving glory to God, [21]and being fully convinced that what He had promised He was also able to perform. [22]And therefore *"it was accounted to him for righteousness."* [23]Now it was not written for his sake alone that it was imputed to him, [24]but also for us. It shall be imputed to us who believe in Him who raised up Jesus our Lord from the dead, [25]who was delivered up because of our

offenses, and was raised because of our justification.

Notice verses 19-22

- Abraham was not weak in faith.
- He did not consider his circumstances.
- He did not waver at the promise of God through unbelief.
- He was strengthened in faith, giving glory (praise) to God, even before he saw the manifestation of what was promised.
- He was FULLY convinced that what God had promised (announced, spoken or professed), He was also able to perform.

Verse 22 goes on to say that, **"it was accounted to him for righteousness."** All Abraham did was believed God, and because of that, it was accounted to him for righteousness!

As believers, we know that God is able to do what He has promised. We know that He is able to do exceedingly, abundantly above all that we ask or think, according to the power that works in us (Ephesians 3:20). We know this, but many times we are not confident or certain that He will do it. God is able and He is willing. He is looking for someone who will take Him at His Word and dare to expect Him to do it. Jesus healed two blind men, but before He healed them, he asked them a question.

Matthew 9:27-29

When Jesus departed from there, two blind men followed Him, crying out and saying, "Son of David, have mercy on us!" **[28] And when He had come into the house, the blind men came to Him. And Jesus said to them, "Do you believe that I am able to do this?" They said to Him, "Yes, Lord." [29] Then He touched their eyes, saying, "According to your faith let it be to you." [30] And their eyes were opened.**

Notice verse 28 said that the blind men came to Him. This implies that if they came to Him, they came desiring and expecting something. Because of the question that Jesus asked them, they knew He was not only able to heal them, but He was also willing to heal them. If they were not confident that He was able to heal them, and if their answer to Him was, "Well Lord, we don't know for certain, but we're just hoping that you can heal us," they would have missed out on their healing. Doubt and unbelief comes from a lack of confidence. When doubt and unbelief is present, then God cannot do what you do not expect Him to do. The Bible says that Jesus could not do mighty works in His own hometown because of their unbelief (Matt. 13:58). They missed out on what was available to them!

The desire of our hearts should be to embrace all that God has for us, and we can! **Hebrews 3:14** tells us how:

"For we have become partakers of Christ if we hold the beginning of our confidence steadfast to the end."

(AMP)
"For we have become fellows with Christ (the Messiah) and share in all He has for us, if only we hold our first newborn confidence and original assured expectation [in virtue of which we are believers] firm and unshaken to the end."

We are to have and to hold…firm and unshaken to the end, **being confident of this very thing, that He who has begun a good work in us will complete it until the day of Jesus Christ (Phil. 1:6).** Praise God!

When we know what is available to us and Whom we have become partakers of, then **we have boldness (courage and confidence) of free access (an unreserved approach to God with freedom and without fear) (Eph. 3:12 AMP).** We have unlimited access to the Father! A lot of internet services charge you a flat fee for unlimited access which many think is pretty reasonable for the wealth of information that is made available to you. Jesus paid the price for us to have unlimited access to the Father, with everything we need at our finger tips (the written Word of God). Everything we will ever need and desire is already on the inside of us. **"He has given us all things that pertain to life and godliness, through the knowledge of Him who called us" (2 Peter 1:3).** We are walking around with wealth, peace, victory, boldness, wisdom…all on the inside of us waiting to be released through our mouths. Having the Word of God as our instruction manual to living a victorious life, the Holy Ghost as our Helper, faith in our hearts, and the ability to create with our mouths, we are well equipped! Our Father not only equipped us, but He has already qualified us to be partakers of the inheritance of the saints (Colossians 1:12). We do not have to earn it nor do we have to beg for it, because we have been made the righteousness of God in Christ Jesus. Praise God!

If our heart does not condemn us, we have confidence toward God, and whatever we ask we receive from Him, because we keep His commandments and do those things that are pleasing in His sight (1 John 3:21-22).

When I first saw this Scripture, I said to the Lord, "You mean to tell me, if I walk in obedience to You and do those things that are pleasing in Your sight, that WHATEVER I ask, I receive?" The Lord responded to me by bringing to my remembrance another Scripture. **"Therefore I say to you, whatever things you ask when you pray, believe that you receive them, and you will have them" (Mark 11:24).** I began to ponder on that one word 'WHATEVER' and I

61

thought, 'this sounds so...so...'UNLIMITED''. I looked up these Scriptures in other translations of the Bible to see if another word was used in place of 'WHATEVER'. I found the word 'ANYTHING'. I then looked up the word 'WHATEVER' in the dictionary and one of the definitions Webster defined it as, was this: "Anything; no matter what."[7] However, we are to look at the Scriptures very closely because all the promises of God in Him are yes, and in Him Amen (2 Cor. 1:20), BUT they are CONDITIONAL. The Word of God tells us that whatever we ask, we receive from Him, but before it said that, there was an 'IF'. IF OUR HEART DOES NOT CONDEMN US, we have confidence towards God, and whatever we ask we receive from Him, BECAUSE WE KEEP HIS COMMANDMENTS AND DO THOSE THINGS THAT ARE PLEASING IN HIS SIGHT (1 John 3:21,22).

1 John 5:14-15

Now this is the confidence that we have in Him, that if we ask anything ACCORDING TO HIS WILL, He hears us.
[15]And if we know that He hears us, whatever we ask, we know that we have the petitions that we have asked of Him.

If you do not know what the will of God is in any given situation, then seek the Lord, trust and expect Him to speak to you concerning the matter. "**...He who comes to**

God must believe that He is, and that He is a rewarder of those who diligently seek Him" (Heb. 11:6). The will of God is always found in the Word of God. If you are not giving time to the Word, then you will be unsure of what His will is. Therefore, you cannot pray with confidence. When you know what the will of God is and have the Word on it, then you can pray with confidence.

Hebrews 10:35-36

Therefore do not cast away your confidence, which has great reward. ³⁶For you have need of endurance, so that after you have done the will of God, you may receive the promise.

3

WAITING IN EXPECTATION

In the morning, O LORD, you hear my voice; in the morning I lay my requests before you and wait in expectation (Psalm 5:3 NIV)

When we are waiting on the Lord, we are to be waiting and resting assured, with the expectancy that what we desire from the Lord, He will bring it to pass. Many times we hear the term 'waiting on the Lord', and we read Scriptures that speak of waiting on the Lord, but we are not to wait on the Lord for the sake of just waiting. We are to wait in expectation, without complaining. To wait means to watch; to stay in a place or remain in readiness or in anticipation until something expected happens.[1]

Our purpose for going to God should not solely be because we want something from Him, but our ultimate purpose should be to know Him. In order to know Him, you have to spend time with Him, just like you would want to spend time with someone you desire to know or have a relationship with. Oftentimes we make the mistake in trying to know someone through someone else. You will then only know 'about' that person, but do not really 'know' the person. To know about someone is to hear information about him or her through someone else. However, to know someone personally involves you spending time with that person, and out of that a relationship is formed. God longs for us to spend time with Him, to commune with Him, therefore making Himself known to us.

In Psalm 5:3, it was obvious that David had a relationship with God. He knew there was something about giving God the first fruit of his day, making his request known to God and waiting in expectation. There is something significant about giving God the first fruit of your day. He should be the first One to Whom we say, "Good morning" to and the last One to Whom we say, "Good night" to. When my children get up in the morning, they look for me to tell me "Good morning". I can not help but to love on them when they do that. I always respond back to them with a hug and a 'good morning'. It is the same when they go to bed at night. They always tell me "Good night", and I always respond with a hug and a 'good night'. If we do that with our children, how much more will God respond to us in a likewise manner. My children are irresistible when they come to me like that. Just the same,

God cannot resist us when we are excited to say, "Good morning" to Him or at the close of the day to say, "Good night" to Him. He longs to respond back to us as well. If we know how to love and give good gifts to our children, how much more will the Father love and give good gifts to us, His children (Matt. 7:11). Remember that He is our example. He was the first lover, and He was the first giver.

We are to wait patiently on the Lord, and in our waiting, we are to rejoice. This is an area where the enemy frequently trips us up. He robs us in our waiting by planting a seed of doubt, which causes us to murmur and complain. We have failed to understand that it is in our waiting (with joyful expectation) that we gain strength. The Bible says in **Isaiah 40:31:**

"But those who wait on the LORD shall renew *their* strength; They shall mount up with wings like eagles, they shall run and not be weary, they shall walk and not faint."

God wants us to rejoice, because the joy of the Lord is our strength. If we do not have any joy in our waiting, then we will not have any strength. If we do not have any strength, then our resistance is low. We will be unable to resist the temptation to faint, give up, throw in the towel and quit. If we faint, give up, throw in the towel and quit, we will never know just how close we were to receiving the promise. As a born again believer, we are destined by God to win. We are destined for victory. **James 1:2-4** says:

"My brethren, count it all joy when you fall into various trials, [3]knowing that the testing of your faith produces patience. [4]But let patience have *its* perfect work, that you may be perfect and complete, lacking nothing."

There are three things we are to learn from these verses:

1) In the midst of all the trials you may be facing, REJOICE! Give God some praise! That word 'joy' comes from the Greek word 'khar-ah', which means calm delight.[2] Therefore rejoice in your waiting, with joyful expectation and at peace in knowing that through faith and patience you will inherit the promise (Heb.6:12).

2) It's a test – a test of your faith, which produces patience (a fruit of the spirit).

3) Be patient! Why? So that it may produce growth in you, strengthening your character, in order for you to become complete (whole), therefore lacking nothing. Now that's being made whole, when you're lacking nothing!

Let's look at the Scriptures again in the book of James 1:2-4, but in a different version (TLB):

Dear brothers, is your life full of difficulties and temptations? Then be happy, ³for when the way is rough, your patience has a chance to grow. ⁴So let it grow, and don't try to squirm out of your problems. For when your patience is finally in full bloom, then you will be ready for anything, strong in character, full and complete.

Even in the midst of a storm, you can still rejoice. It is an act of your will. Your attitude plays a big part of what your outcome will be. Therefore, it is very important that you maintain the right attitude in whatever you may be facing. However, it is imperative that you stay in faith. Happiness should not be based on material things or what we have or do not have. It is a choice. I choose to be happy. Why? Because of Who I know and believe, who I am in Him, and knowing what He has made available to me through my inheritance. My inheritance exist because of the covenant made to me being that I am a joint heir with Christ, a seed of Abraham and a child of the Most High God! Now that's something to rejoice and be happy about!

Romans 12:12 (NIV) says, "Be joyful in hope (joyful expectation), patient in affliction, faithful in prayer."

Apostle Paul said in **Romans 8:18,19 (KJV):**

"For I reckon that the sufferings of this present time are not worthy to be compared with the glory which shall be revealed in us. [19]For the earnest expectation of the creature waiteth for the manifestation of the sons of God."

The Word says that the whole creation is waiting with intense anticipation, expectantly and patiently for the manifestation or the revealing of the sons of God. It will happen, and it is happening. Why? Because the whole creation is expecting it! Faith and expectation will always produce manifestation.

Paul goes on to say further in the latter part of verse 24 and 25:

"But hope that is seen is no hope at all. Who hopes for what he already has? [25]But if we hope for what we do not yet have, we wait for it patiently."

There is peace, strength and an inheritance made available to us if we learn to wait in expectation. We should make it a lifestyle to live in a continual state of expectancy.

Psalm 37:3-11

[3] **Trust in the LORD, and do good;**

70

Dwell in the land, and feed on His faithfulness.

4 Delight yourself also in the LORD,
And He shall give you the desires of your heart.

5 Commit your way to the LORD,
Trust also in Him,
And He shall bring *it* to pass.

6 He shall bring forth your righteousness as the light,
And your justice as the noonday.

7 Rest in the LORD, and wait patiently for Him;
Do not fret because of him who prospers in his way,
Because of the man who brings wicked schemes to pass.

8 Cease from anger, and forsake wrath;
Do not fret—*it* only *causes* harm.

9 For evildoers shall be cut off;
But those who wait on the LORD,
They shall inherit the earth.

10 For yet a little while and the wicked *shall be* no *more;*
Indeed, you will look carefully for his place,
But it *shall be* no *more.*

11 But the meek shall inherit the earth,
And shall delight themselves in the abundance of peace.

We are to trust in the Lord, delight ourselves in the Lord, commit our ways to the Lord, rest in the Lord and joyfully wait patiently in expectation on the Lord. Why? Because those who wait in expectancy shall inherit the earth, and shall delight themselves in the abundance of peace. Where there is peace, there will be rest. What does it mean to rest in the Lord? It simply means to quiet self; to be still. In other words, it means to stop struggling.

The Trap of the Enemy

The Bible tells us to not be ignorant of the enemy's devices (2 Cor.2:11). Jesus uncovers his purpose in **John 10:10: The thief** (enemy) **does not come except to steal, and to kill, and to destroy. I have come that they may have life, and that they may have it more abundantly.**

We see here that we *had* a problem, and we **have** the answer. Whenever there is a problem, there is always an answer, and the answer is always found in the Word of God. However, one of our greatest enemies is ignorance. If the enemy can keep us out of the Word by robbing us of our time and causing us to become too busy, he knows we are harmless to him. It is important to make time for the Word of God, making it a priority in our lives, because it is our lives. Through ignorance, the enemy can steal the abundant life that God so freely made available to us. The word 'may' in John 10:10 tells me that there are some that may or may not have 'life more abundantly'. In order to have this abundant life, it has to be received. You cannot receive something you do not know that you have. So the enemy steals it from them without them knowing it. It is done through a lack of knowledge…ignorance. That is the enemy's whole objective, to steal something from you (that you did not know you had), kill something in you (your dream or your destiny), and finally to destroy your faith through doubt, unbelief and discouragement. The underlying fact is that he has many tools that he uses, such as strife, offense, unforgiveness, lust, and many others, but a lie is the handle that fits them all. The Bible describes him in **John 8:44** as **a murderer and that he does not stand in the truth, because there is no truth in him. When he speaks a lie, he speaks from his own resources, for he is a liar and the father of it.**

You will not recognize his lies if you don't know what the Word says, because circumstances will make what you see or think appear real. Every time the enemy approached Jesus, Jesus always overcame him by speaking the Word (Luke 4). **Hosea 4:6** (NIV) says, **"My people are destroyed from a lack of knowledge."** The enemy knows if he can keep you ignorant, you will never know what is rightfully yours.

Many times we are so easily discouraged when things do not turn out the way we want or planned. A lot of times we are not encouraged until we see something good happen. Sometimes we do not see the manifestation of the promises of God in our lives because we become discouraged in our waiting. This is one of the biggest traps of the enemy. The strategy is to cause you to get discouraged by listening to his lies and applying some pressure to tempt you to give up and in the end abort the promise. The Word is sown in our hearts and we become pregnant with a dream, vision or a promise from God. After carrying it for a while, we then become weary when we do not see any progress, which oftentimes result in abortion. The Word of God says in **Galatians 6:9:**

"And let us not grow weary while doing good, for in due season we shall reap if we do not lose heart."

If the Word says that we shall reap IF we do not lose heart, then you can bank on it! Your circumstances should never dictate your actions. We are to live by faith and respond in faith, with the expectancy that we are going to reap if we faint not. That means you do not cave in under pressure, throw in the towel or quit. When you are tempted to get discouraged, do not wait to tell your problem to others, hoping to get some encouragement from them. Don't misunderstand me, we are to exhort one another daily, while it is called "Today" (Heb. 3:13). However, there comes a time when you have to learn to encourage yourself. How do you encourage yourself? By speaking the Word to yourself. You have to talk to yourself and build yourself up. Jude speaks of this in verse 20:

74

"But you, beloved, building yourselves up on your most holy faith, praying in the Holy Spirit."

When you pray in the Holy Spirit, you will find yourself being strengthened. Scriptures will start coming to you and as you began to pray the Word, the Word will come alive on the inside of you being full of power, making it active, operative, energizing and effective (Hebrews 4:12 AMP). **The earnest heartfelt continued prayer of a righteous man makes tremendous power available, dynamic in its working (James 5:16b AMP).** There is power activated when we pray in the Holy Spirit, and the Holy Spirit will quicken us to pray the Word.

Whatever comes, do not abort the promise or the dream that God gave you. If God said it, it will come to pass. There is always a due season and an appointed time. The part you play is to stay in faith, stay focused, wait patiently and expectantly for the manifestation of whatever you are believing God for. Don't fall into the trap of the enemy and receive the seed of doubt and unbelief by listening to his lies.

When you begin to speak contrary to the Word, murmuring, complaining and becoming discouraged, you have already been snared. The good news is that you don't have to stay there. You can come out of that and be free! It is the truth that you know, understand and apply that will make you free. Start speaking truth, which is the Word of God. David said in **Psalm 27:13,14:**

"I would have lost heart, **unless I had believed that I would see the goodness of the LORD in the land of the living."**

David was saying that he would have lost heart or fainted, gave up or quit, unless he had believed and expected to see the goodness of the Lord.

Then he encourages us to:

[14]**Wait** (in expectancy) **on the LORD; be of good courage** (strong; by being constant, encouraging self), **and He shall strengthen your heart; wait** (in expectancy), **I say, on the LORD!**

There is a story in 1 Samuel, chapter 30 that speaks of David's conflict with the Amalekites. Look at what David does:

Now it happened, when David and his men came to Ziklag, on the third day, that the Amalekites had invaded the South and Ziklag, attacked Ziklag and burned it with fire, [2]**and had taken captive the women and those who** *were* **there, from small to great; they did not kill anyone, but carried** *them* **away and went their way.**

76

³So David and his men came to the city, and there it was, burned with fire; and their wives, their sons, and their daughters had been taken captive. <u>⁴Then David and the people who *were* with him lifted up their voices and wept, until they had no more power to weep.</u> ⁵And David's two wives, Ahinoam the Jezreelitess, and Abigail the widow of Nabal the Carmelite, had been taken captive. <u>⁶Now David was greatly distressed, for the people spoke of stoning him, because the soul of all the people was grieved, every man for his sons and his daughters. But David strengthened himself in the LORD his God.</u> ⁷Then David said to Abiathar the priest, Ahimelech's son, "Please bring the ephod here to me." And Abiathar brough the ephod to David. <u>⁸So David inquired of the LORD, saying, "Shall I pursue this troop? Shall I overtake them?"</u> <u>And He answered him, "Pursue, for you shall surely overtake *them* and without fail recover *all*."</u> <u>⁹So David went,</u> he and the six hundred men who *were* with him, and came to the Brook Besor, where those stayed who were left behind. <u>¹⁰But David pursued...</u> ¹⁹And nothing of theirs was lacking, either small or great, sons or daughters, spoil or anything which they had taken from them; <u>David recovered all.</u>

Notice in verse 4, that David and the people who were with him cried until they drained themselves of their strength. They could not cry anymore. In verse 6, David became discouraged, and on top of that, the people spoke of stoning him. They began to turn against David because of their grief. The Scripture goes on to say in verse 6 that David strengthened (encouraged) himself in the Lord. No one offered him any encouragement because they were discouraged themselves, but David turned to God. Before he made a decision, he inquired of the Lord. By encouraging himself, I believe David came to a place of remembrance. He remembered God's faithfulness in times past. In verse 8, David asked God if he should pursue the troop and overtake them. God answered David, and told him what to do, and then gave him a promise. The promise was that he would overtake them and without fail recover all. In verse 9, David went. You can rest assured that he went with the expectancy that what God had promised, he was able to perform. In verse 10, it says that David pursued, and in verse 19, it says that David recovered all.

When David inquired of the Lord, I believe he expected to hear from God. He was no longer discouraged, because he had encouraged himself in the Lord. Encouragement always brings strength. If David had not arose, encouraged himself and inquired of the Lord, he and the people would have never experienced the victory and the blessing that came along with it. They would have missed out because they would have fainted, given up, threw in the towel and quit.

Discouragement is a trap of the enemy to get us to give up. Discouragement brings weakness, but encouragement brings strength. The enemy knows if he can keep us discouraged, we will not have the energy or the strength to fight. We would no longer be a threat to him in doing the kingdom of darkness damage.

Habakkuk encouraged himself even when everything else failed, he trusted in God's salvation.

Habakkuk 3:17-19

[17] **Though the fig tree may not blossom,**
    Nor fruit be on the vines;
  Though the labor of the olive may fail,
   And the fields yield no food;
   Though the flock may be cut off from the fold,
   And there be no herd in the stalls—
[18] **Yet I will rejoice in the LORD,**
   I will joy in the God of my salvation.
[19] **The LORD God is my strength;**
   He will make my feet like deer's *feet*,
   And He will make me walk on my high hills.

Habakkuk was saying, "No matter what happens, I'm going to rejoice in the Lord, because the joy of the Lord is my strength." For him to go on to say, "He will make my feet like deer's feet, and He will make me walk on my high hills," he had to expect it. God wants us to get to a place in Him, that when everything seems to go wrong, we can still be encouraged and confident in knowing that **all things work together for good to those who love God, to those who are called according to His purpose (Rom. 8:28)**. That's why it is very important to get rooted and grounded in the Word of God, so that when things happen contrary to what you may want, the Word on the inside of you will rise up in you. You will then be able to grab hold to it and encourage yourself. Once you are encouraged, you can be an encouragement to others.

If you do not feed your spirit the Word of God, when fear, worry, anxiety, discouragement, doubt and unbelief comes, it will overtake you and cause you to make hasty decisions based on your circumstances and not based on what the Word says. When the Word of God is in your heart and upon your lips, you can overcome all those things.

Yet in all these things we are more than conquerors through Him who loved us (Romans 8:37).

We are to live by faith, not by sight. Do not let circumstances change you, but you change the circumstances. It is not important what happens on the outside as much as what's happening on the inside of you.

What happens on the inside of you will affect your world on the outside. You have the power to frame and change your world by speaking in faith the Word of God.

Staying Focused

No matter what challenges you may be facing, it is imperative that you stay focused on the Word of God and your expected end. It's easy sometimes to become distracted in your waiting on the Lord. In the book of Proverbs, wisdom cries out to get us to focus on and take heed to the counsel that wisdom is giving. The word 'wisdom' is used throughout the book of Proverbs, but also know this – wherever you see the word 'wisdom' you can also refer to it as 'The Word of God'. The Word of God is wisdom, and God's wisdom is His Word. When you need the wisdom of God in any situation, it is just the same as you needing the Word of the Lord. **Wisdom** (the Word of God) **is the principal thing; therefore get wisdom** (the Word of God), **and in all your getting, get understanding (Proverbs 4:7)**. Once you receive the wisdom of God, obstacles or trials may come, but the key to victory is to stay focused on what you have received from God, and having done all to stand, stand! The ability to stay focused is one of the most needful and the most successful skills you can ever have and develop. To maintain the proper focus, you will

81

have to stay in the Word, stay in constant fellowship with God and with other believers, stay in faith, walk in love and joyfully wait in expectation, even in the midst of adversity. Improper focus is a result of focusing on the problem, which will cause you to make a hasty decision based on the circumstances rather than the Word or the wisdom of God. You would have chosen a way that seemed right, but in the end it will lead to ruin (Proverbs 14:12). There is a path of the wicked and there is a path of the just. Taking hold of and walking in wisdom will keep you on the right path, but this will only happen if you stay focused.

Proverbs 4:10-27 speaks of this:

10   **Hear, my son, and receive my sayings,**
     And the years of your life will be many.
11   **I have taught you in the way of wisdom;**
     I have led you in right paths.
12   **When you walk, your steps will not be hindered,**
     And when you run, you will not stumble.
13   **Take firm hold of instruction, do not let go;**
     Keep her, for she *is* your life.
14   **Do not enter the path of the wicked,**
     And do not walk in the way of evil.
15   **Avoid it, do not travel on it;**
     Turn away from it and pass on.

¹⁶ For they do not sleep unless they have done evil;
And their sleep is taken away unless they make someone fall.

¹⁷ For they eat the bread of wickedness,
And drink the wine of violence.

¹⁸ But the path of the just *is* like the shining sun,
That shines ever brighter unto the perfect day.

¹⁹ The way of the wicked *is* like darkness;
They do not know what makes them stumble.

²⁰ My son, give attention to my words;
Incline your ear to my sayings.

²¹ Do not let them depart from your eyes (stay focused on them);
Keep them in the midst of your heart;

²² For they *are* life to those who find them,
And health to all their flesh.

²³ Keep your heart with all diligence,
For out of it *spring* the issues of life.

²⁴ Put away from you a deceitful mouth,
And put perverse lips far from you.

²⁵ Let your eyes look straight ahead (stay focused),
And your eyelids look right before you.

²⁶ Ponder the path of your feet,
And let all your ways be established.

²⁷ Do not turn to the right or the left (stay focused);
Remove your foot from evil.

There is security in wisdom. Can you hear wisdom crying out? Wisdom is telling us to take hold of her (instruction), guard our hearts, watch the words of our mouths, stay focused and watch the path of our feet. The key here is to stay focused on the instruction that is given. It is your life!

One of my hobbies is photography. When I want a nice clear crisp picture, I have to make sure that the camera is set and I am focused on the subject. If I am distracted in any way I might lose time, the right moment and I will have to begin again by refocusing on the subject and hope for another opportunity for a great picture. My goal is to capture on film the subject at the right moment. If the object of my attention moves, then I have to keep my eyes on the subject by staying focused until I capture on film the desired picture. Whatever I'm focusing on, that's what will develop. If my focus is blurred, then I have to make the necessary adjustments to get a clear picture. I may have to change my position, even if it is uncomfortable. It may be uncomfortable but it is necessary. Sometimes photographers and cameramen have to get on their knees or stand in an awkward position just to get a good picture. They will do whatever it takes to get that perfect shot. My rule of getting a good picture is this – Focusing is the principal thing, therefore focus, but in all your focusing, get a clear picture. In our everyday life, we need directions or instructions, but to follow directions or instructions you need wisdom and understanding. **Wisdom is the principal** thing, therefore get wisdom, and in all your getting, get understanding (Proverbs 4:7). Understanding will give you a clear picture. In order to stay focused on the Word of God and what He says or gives you to do, you have to be willing to do what it takes to stay focused, even if it's uncomfortable.

Distractions are assignments to cause you to lose your focus. **Hebrews 12:1-2 says:**

"...let us lay aside every weight, and the sin which so easily ensnares us, and let us run with endurance the race that is set before us, looking unto Jesus, the author and finisher of our faith, who for the joy that was set before Him endured the cross, despising the shame, and has sat down at the right hand of the throne of God."

The Amplified Version says in verse 2: "**Looking away [from all that will distract]...**"

Jesus endured the cross because He was focused on the will of the Father. Thank God He was focused! We have to follow in that same pattern. Apostle Paul tells us in 2 Timothy 2:3-5:

"You therefore must endure hardship as a good soldier of Jesus Christ. ⁴No one engaged in warfare entangles himself with the affairs of *this* life, that he may please him who

enlisted him as a soldier." Why? Because he is focused!
⁵"And also if anyone competes in athletics, he is not crowned
unless he competes according to the rules."

We are to focus on doing the will of the Father and
looking unto Jesus and away from all that will distract.
Satan is seriously threatened when the people of God are
focused. People that are focused are determined to win.
They are determined to fulfill their purpose and reach their
goal. The Apostle Paul was a focused man. No matter what
the circumstances were, he remained the same. He did not
waver, compromise, nor did he allow himself to become
distracted. This is why he could say with confidence,
"...I have fought the good fight, I have finished the race, I
have kept the faith" (2 Timothy 4:7). It should be our goal
as well – to finish the race by keeping the faith. Apostle
Paul did not look back, but he stayed focused by pressing
forward. The enemy will always try to get us to look back.
He knows that you cannot press or move forward looking
back. Just as Apostle Paul did, we have to forget those
things which are behind and reach forward to those things
which are ahead. We have to continue to stand and
continue pressing toward the goal (Phil.3:13,14). Any
successful athlete will tell you that staying focused
contributed to their success as well as training hard. It takes
discipline to stay focused. A runner who runs in a race is
trained to focus on the finish line. He knows if he gives in

to the temptation of looking back to see where his opponent is, it may cost him the race.

Anytime my husband and I were challenged by trials, faced with obstacles or believed God for something, we would always run to the Word of God to see what God had to say about it. We would do all we knew to do according to the Word and then we would stand. We knew and understood the importance of staying focused on what we had received from God, regardless of the circumstances. In staying focused on the Word of God, which is the wisdom or the will of God, and living according to the Word, we have always seen the goodness of God. God's Word has never failed. In due season, the promise of God manifested in our lives over and over again. There have been times when we had to adjust or change and refocus, but each time, we were determined to keep speaking the Word. We continued to walk in love and we were determined not to give up, but to fulfill the purpose in which God has called us. In this, God has always caused us to triumph and manifestation was always inevitable.

The temptation to give in to discouragement, especially in our waiting on the Lord, can be eliminated by staying focused. There is hope and there is help available. The Word is our hope and the Holy Ghost is our Helper. He will help us in every area of our lives, even in helping us to stay focused, if we let Him.

"But the Comforter (Counselor, Helper, Intercessor, Advocate, Strengthener, Standby), the Holy Spirit, Whom the Father will send in My name [in My place, to represent Me and act on My behalf], He will teach you all things. And He will cause you to recall (will remind you of, bring to your remembrance) everything I have told you." (John 14:26).

4

YOUR EXPECTED END

For I know the thoughts that I think toward you, saith the LORD, thoughts of peace, and not of evil, to give you an expected end (Jeremiah 29:11 KJV).

It should be comforting for us to know that God is always thinking about us, and all of His thoughts, plans and purposes towards us are all good. He has thoughts of peace towards us. The word 'peace' in this Scripture has a broad meaning. It means welfare, that is, (good) health, prosperity, favor, rest, safety, wellness, and wholeness.[1] God wants us to have everything He destined and purposed us to have. Let's look at the same Scripture, but in another translation:

"For I know the plans I have for you, declares the LORD, plans to prosper you and not to harm you, plans to give you hope and a future" (NIV).

God has plans for us, plans to prosper us and not to harm us. It's amazing how He gets blamed for a lot of harm that

He did not bring upon people or upon the earth. Some people were told that it was God Who made them sick, in order to teach them something. Some were told that it was simply not God's will to heal them or to prosper them in order to humble them. The truth of the matter is that God wants us well and prosperous. It is His will and His plan for us. We hear of the destruction of thunderstorms, tornadoes and hurricanes and it is said to be 'acts of God'. God is not a God of destruction. Jesus said in **John 10:10**:

"The thief does not come except to steal, and to kill, and to destroy. I have come that they may have life, and that they may have *it* more abundantly."

Jesus and the disciples got into a boat with the mission to cross over to the other side, but suddenly a storm arose as He slept. The disciples panicked and cried out in fear, and Jesus was awakened. **"Then He arose and rebuked the wind, and said to the sea, "Peace, be still!" And the wind ceased and there was a great calm"(Mark 4:39).** Now if storms, tornadoes and hurricanes were acts of God, why would He rebuke the winds and the waves when He was with the disciples? You may say, "Well that was then, this is now." He is the same yesterday, today and forever, praise God! (Heb. 13:8).

In Matthew 12:24-27, Jesus was accused by the

Pharisees of casting out demons by Beelzebub (of Chaldee origin; a name of Satan).[2]

[25]But Jesus knew their thoughts, and said to them: "Every kingdom divided against itself is brought to desolation, and every city or house divided against itself will not stand. [26]If Satan casts out Satan, he is divided against himself. How then will his kingdom stand? [27]And if I cast out demons by Beelzebub, by whom do your sons cast them out? Therefore they shall be your judges. [28]But if I cast out demons by the Spirit of God, surely the kingdom of God has come upon you."

So you see, God could not cause a storm and then rebuke the storm or cast out a demon by the name of Satan. He would then be divided against Himself, and there is no division in God. He was acting in His own authority, which He has now given to us.

God's plan for us is not for our destruction or harm. His plan is to give us hope and a future, an expected end. In every circumstance and situation, think about what you want the end result to be, then in faith speak the end result and nothing more, without looking back. When Jesus rebuked the fig tree, He was confident in the authority His words carried. He did not look back to see if what He said was going to happen. He spoke the end result and kept going (Mark 11:13-14, 21,22). You will be operating in the same principle and authority that Jesus operated in, calling those things which do not exist as though they did (Rom. 4:17). Faith always speaks and leaves no room for doubt. Faith believes that those things it says will be done (Mark 11:23). Your faith, hope and expectation will produce for you the manifestation of your expected end.

Proverbs 23:17-18 (AMP)

Let not your heart envy sinners, but continue in the reverent and worshipful fear of the Lord all the day long. For surely there is a latter end [a future and a reward], and your hope and expectation shall not be cut off.

The words '*cut off*' denotes to be destroyed or consumed; specifically to covenant; to cut, fail, be forgotten, hew down, perish, or lost.[3] There is an expected end (a future), a reward of your expectation. Your hope and expectation shall not be destroyed or consumed. It shall not fail or be forgotten because of the covenant. Whatever you expect, that is what your end will be.

God has given each one of us a measure of faith, but it is up to us what we do with the measure that we are given. He expects us to use what we have, and He expects us to develop it. When God invested in us, He expected increase.

Our faith can be developed and increased by studying and meditating on the Word of God, listening to tapes, fellowshipping with the Lord and with your sisters and brothers in Christ. Start working out by exercising your faith until you become a spiritual Clint Eastwood. Then when the devil shows up at your door and threaten to put sickness on you, you can stand firm in faith and say, "Come on devil, make my day," and then bust him in the mouth with the Word! He will flee from you in terror. Don't be intimidated by the enemy with his threats in the form of circumstances. When you speak boldly the Word of God in faith, then expect results. Once you come into the knowledge of the truth, you can walk in the freedom and victory that God has predestined you to walk in. It is the truth that you know, understand and apply that will make you free.

When I was a young girl, I battled with a severe skin disorder called 'Eczema'. It was so bad growing up until I would try to hide the terrible rashes it left all over my body with extra clothing. In the summer, I would wear thin cotton long sleeve shirts, and I would hardly ever wear shorts. I was always called names in Junior High School, like 'alligator woman' or 'the skin monster'. I would itch so badly and it seemed that medicines and different cremes I was prescribed never worked. I remember buying a hairbrush just to scratch with. It was the only temporary relief that worked, but it left me scarred. Once I graduated from high school and went off to college, I began to research this skin disorder. I would spend hours in the library, desperate to find some answers and some relief. The only answers I found was this particular skin disorder was hereditary, and there was no cure, only treatment. Well I knew about the treatments, but they did not work for me. I became discouraged and frustrated. I wanted to wear short sleeve shirts, shorts and go swimming without people noticing my rashes. They did not want to get in the pool if I was in it.

It wasn't long before I received Jesus Christ as Lord after being invited to a church service on campus. I became hungry for the Word of God. I was hungry for truth. There was still a longing in my heart to get some relief from this skin disorder. I heard about healing and that Jesus paid the price for my healing, but how do I lay hold of it? How do I get the manifestation of my healing? This was my heart's cry. I was prayed for, but nothing happened. I didn't really expect anything to happen, but I was just hoping that it would. The devil would attack my mind with the thought, "You don't expect for it to just go away, do you? Besides, you've had this problem all your life." I believed his lie, until I came into the knowledge of the truth of God's Word, the finish work on the cross. I began to bask in the presence of God and search the Scriptures concerning my healing. I was led to read Isaiah 53. It was loaded! I saw it in the Word! I got real excited because revelation had come. It was my answer! I knew that I did not have to live with this skin disorder anymore. I received my healing by faith, and I expected manifestation. I began to rejoice! I knew healing was mine!

Isaiah 53:4-5:

4 **Surely He has borne our griefs**
And carried our sorrows;
Yet we esteemed Him stricken,
Smitten by God, and afflicted.
5 **But He *was* wounded for our transgressions,**
***He was* bruised for our iniquities;**
The chastisement for our peace *was* upon Him,
And by His stripes we are healed.

I was even more excited because I had a cross-reference in my Bible and it led me to **1 Peter 2:24**:

...Who Himself bore our sins in His own body on the tree, that we, having died to sins, might live for righteousness—by whose stripes you were healed.

I focused on these two passages of Scriptures. I knew it

was not the will of God for me to suffer like I did or else He would not have sent Jesus to suffer in my place. Jesus going to the cross in my place would have been useless. I knew I had ammunition in my mouth, and all I had to do was pull the trigger—speaking the Word of God in faith, declaring my healing. I was excited about receiving what was already mine. No matter what anyone said and saw, they could not talk me out of my healing. Healing was mine! I kept those two Scriptures before me and meditated on them day and night. When I started to itch I would say, "Lord, I thank you for my healing and I thank you for the manifestation of my healing. I thank you that this itch has got to go and I receive relief from it now in the name of Jesus." I did not know when I would see the manifestation, but I expected it, which was enough to keep me rejoicing.

It wasn't long after that, before my faith and expectation brought forth the manifestation of my healing. Not only was I healed, but I was also made whole! You may say, "What's the difference?" The difference is, if I was only healed, then I would be free from all the discomforts that this disorder brought, but I would still have the scars from it. To be made whole would be with nothing missing, no discomforts and no signs of this disease. So you see, not only did God heal me, but He also removed the ugly scars that it left on my body! I was made whole! He's a God that is more than enough! Therefore if the Son made me free, then I am free indeed! (John 8:36). Today, I am still enjoying that freedom, because I had received my expected end.

Your Testimony

The word 'testimony', is any affirmation or declaration; any form of evidence; record or report given.[4] Your testimony is another one of the most powerful tools you will ever have and the enemy knows it. He has kept many of God's people silent for too long. Your testimony is never really about you, but it is all about Him. The devil knows that your testimony will challenge you to press forward, being fruitful in every good work, increasing in the knowledge of God and impacting the lives of others. That is why he creates distractions in your life, to get you off course and to keep you silent. A testimony is not always after the fact, but it is our affirmation or declaration before the fact. It is the spirit of prophecy (Rev. 19:10). Prophesy to your situation, and speak the Word of God with boldness, expecting it to turn out for your good. Don't speak anything contrary to that prophecy, so that it will become a reality, and then you will have a testimony! God needs you and wants you to give testimony of Him. Why?

Because there are others that need your testimony. If He is lifted up (in your testimony), He will draw all men unto Himself (John 12:32). God is glorified in your testimony.

Revelation 12:11 says:

"And they overcame him by the blood of the Lamb and by the word of their testimony, and they did not love their lives to the death."

One of the definitions of the word 'word' in this Scripture comes from the Greek word 'lego', which simply means to break silence.[5] No matter how great or small you think your testimony is, break the silence and give your testimony! Let the redeemed of the LORD say so! (Psalm 107:2). The power of God is released through the word of your testimony. The gospel is revealed, even in your testimony. Therefore, do not hide the gospel. Apostle Paul said in 2 Corinthians 4:3, **"If our gospel be hid, it is hid to them that are lost" (KJV).** David said in Psalm 96:2b-3: **"…Proclaim the good news of His salvation from day to day. [3]Declare His glory among the nations, His wonders among all peoples."**

Because the blood has already been shed signifies that the devil has already been defeated, and we need to give testimony to that. It is also a reminder to us that he is defeated. Oftentimes we have drifted away from sharing the goodness of God by focusing too much on our problems. Sometimes God wants to take us back in order to move us forward. He wants us to remember our past victories. The way I got through some of the things I faced was by remembering how God delivered and helped me in times past. I remembered my past victories and it built my faith and confidence in knowing that whatever I was facing, He would bring me through. I then expected God to work in my behalf. If we would remember and meditate on the things God brought us through, we would be aware of His willingness to work in our present situation as well. We would see it as another opportunity to have the power of God manifested in our lives, creating another testimony to make known His goodness. David said in **Psalm 63:6,7:**

6 **"When I remember You on my bed,**
   I meditate on You in the *night* watches.
7 **Because You have been my help,**
   Therefore in the shadow of Your wings I will rejoice."

David was able to rejoice in whatever state he was in because he remembered that God had been his help in times before. When we become anxious or worried, it is because we have forgotten that God has been our help in times past. **He is our refuge and strength, a very present help in trouble (Psalm 46:1).** Even in the times of trouble, it does not compare to the glory that will be revealed in us. Apostle Paul said in **Romans 8:18:**

"For I consider that the sufferings of this present time are not worthy *to be compared* with the glory which shall be revealed in us."

The glory of God is the presence and the power of God being manifested through us by signs, wonders, through the working of miracles and through the word of our testimony.
.

In Psalm 78, the children of Israel were repeatedly remembering the works of God and then forgetting. This provoked, grieved and limited Him. They did not remember God's power nor the day when He redeemed them from the hand of the enemy (verse 42,43). They should have spoken of His goodness, instead of complaining. This would have encouraged them to continue in following after God, regardless of the circumstances. Even in their rebellion and unfaithfulness to God, He was still faithful.

Anytime we remember God, He shows up on the scene. Jonah was in the belly of a fish three days and three nights. He became discouraged. He said, **"When my soul fainted within me, I remembered the Lord" (Jonah 2:7).** In his remembering the Lord he prayed, and God heard him and spoke to the fish, and the fish vomited Jonah onto dry land. When God answered Jonah, it was a result of him remembering the Lord. When we remember the goodness of God, it is important that we open our mouths and declare His goodness. There are others that need to know the goodness and the power of God.

If a man was paralyzed in a wheel chair, and God miraculously healed him, for a stranger to see him in a store would mean nothing to that stranger. But if the man shared with the stranger how God miraculously healed him, then he would have the stranger's attention, especially if the stranger was also paralyzed and in a wheel chair. The stranger may never know the healing power of God, if the man that God miraculously healed keeps silent. You may not know whom God wants to reach through your testimony, but be willing to give it. Your testimony may not be as dramatic as that, but it does not matter, the goodness of God is still revealed. Don't let the enemy lie and convince you that you do not have a testimony unless it is something dramatic. His plan is to keep you silent. He does not want you to impart hope to someone else or impact someone else's life with your testimony. Every time Jesus healed someone, He either told them to go and show themselves as a testimony or the news of what He had done, spread throughout the land. Lives were changed because someone testified of what Jesus had done

(Matt.8:4). Look at what David says in Psalm 145. What he declared, we are now seeing:

Psalm 145: 4-7,10-12:

4 **One generation shall praise Your works to another,**
   And shall declare Your mighty acts.
5 **I will meditate on the glorious splendor of Your majesty,**
   And on Your wondrous works.
6 ***Men* shall speak of the might of Your awesome acts,**
   And I will declare Your greatness.
7 **They shall utter the memory of Your great goodness,**
   And shall sing of Your righteousness.
10 **All Your works shall praise You, O LORD,**
   And Your saints shall bless You.
11 **They shall speak of the glory of Your kingdom,**
   And talk of Your power,
12 **To make known to the sons of men His mighty acts,**
   And the glorious majesty of His kingdom.

Prophesy and Testify!

It's All Good

God is a good God and because He is a good God, His thoughts and plans towards us are all good (Jer. 29:11). Psalm 145 speaks of this. He:

- is gracious towards us
- is full of compassion
- is slow to anger
- is of great mercy
- is good to all
- satisfies the desire of every living thing
- is near to all who call on Him
- fulfills the desire of them that fear Him
- will hear our cry and save us
- preserves all who love Him

This is the picture that God wants us to have of Him. When we thank Him for His goodness, His response is "You're welcome, it is My pleasure." Everything that He does for us or through us, it's for our good and His pleasure. **"For it is God who works in you both to will and to do for His good pleasure" (Phil. 2:13).** It pleases the Father to be at work in us. It is also the Father's good pleasure to give us the Kingdom (Luke 12:32). He takes pleasure, even in our prosperity! (Psalm 35:27). Therefore, we can expect good things from Him and He expects good things from us, because He has invested Himself in us. His investments are all good!

When I look at my daughter, sometimes I can see some resemblance of me in her. She even reminds me of myself.

In the same way, God looks at us and He see Himself. Can you imagine God saying to you, "You remind me of Me." It is so important to see ourselves the way He sees us. Once we see ourselves right, we will begin to see others right. As the people of God, we can not afford to give up on ourselves nor can we afford to give up on others. To give up on others or even ourselves is to give up on God. God can not give up on us because He would then have given up on Himself, and He cannot deny Himself. He began a good work in us, and He expects to complete it (Phil.1:6). He has an expected end awaiting us. Besides, He is the One Who declared, **"I am the Alpha and the Omega, the Beginning and the End" (Rev.1:8).** That tells me that He is not finished with us. He is bringing us into completion and will perfect that which concerns us (Psalm 138:8). So you see, it's all good! No matter what happens in our lives, we can expect it to turn out for our good, because the Word said it would (Rom. 8:28). **Psalm 34:19 (NIV) says, "A righteous man may have many troubles, BUT the Lord delivers him from them all.** That tells me that trouble does not last always, Praise God! We have a Rescuer! So you see, we are surrounded with the goodness of God. **"Oh, taste and see that the Lord is good; Blessed is the man who trusts in Him!" (Psalm 34:8).**

God loves us so much that He gave, and He never stopped giving. If we are to live by faith, then He expects us to expect from Him, because our expectation is from Him (Psalm 62:5). He does not want us to be in want or in need for anything. It is God Who promised to supply all our needs according to His riches in glory by Christ Jesus (Phil. 4:19). That means that He is our source. It is a good thing to stay connected to the source, our lifeline. It is NOT a good thing to look to our jobs as our source, no matter how much we earn. That job is only a means, and can cut you off at their discretion, no matter how much you may want to abide there. But Jesus said, **"If you abide in Me, and My words abide in you, you will ask what you desire and it shall be done for you" (John 15:7).** You may wonder or fill unsure about the future of your job, but you can rest assured that if you stay connected to the Vine, there is a sure future and an expected end. You can ask what you desire and it shall be done for you. No good thing will He withhold from those who walk uprightly (Psalm 84:11b). He will give what is good (Psalm 85:12a). He daily loads us with benefits (Psalm 68:19). Because no one can say this about his or her job, then it would be unwise to make it your source. **"But seek first the kingdom of God and His righteousness, and all these things shall be added to you" (Matt.6:33).** Those who seek the Lord shall not lack any good thing (Psalm 34:10). Even if you have a stressful job, by trusting in Him and His ability, you can live above the effects of stress. Everything we need or desire, we are to look to Him as our source.

Matthew 11:28-30 (AMP) says:

"Come to Me, all you who labor and are heavy-laden and overburdened, and I will cause you to rest. [I will ease and relieve and refresh your souls.] Take My yoke upon you and learn of Me, for I am gentle (meek) and humble (lowly) in heart, and you will find rest (relief and ease and refreshment and recreation and blessed quiet) for your souls. For My yoke is wholesome (useful, good - not harsh, hard, sharp, or pressing, but comfortable, gracious, and pleasant, and My burden is light and easy to be borne."

No matter how difficult life can be at times, it is never as bad as it seems. God wants us to come to Him, and when we do, He is eager to answer. Expect Him to answer. Because expectation is a breeding ground for miracles, we need to cultivate expectancy in every area of our lives. Expect to prosper. Expect God's favor to be upon you. Expect to walk in divine health. Expect to reap a harvest on your seed sown. Expect change in your circumstances. Expect restoration. Expect the desires of your heart to be fulfilled. Live in a continual state of expectancy.

"Because he has set his love upon Me, therefore I will deliver him; I will set him on high, because he has known My name. He shall call upon Me, and I will answer him; I will be with him in trouble; I will deliver him and honor him. With long life I will satisfy him, and show him My salvation" (Psalm 91:14-16).

Blessed be the Lord God, the God of Israel, Who only does wondrous things!

(Psalm 72:18)

Because He is a good God, It's all good! Therefore, live expectantly!

ENDNOTES

Chapter 1

[1] Strong's Hebrew and Greek Dictionary G4102
[2] Strong's Hebrew and Greek Dictionary G1680
[1] Webster's New World Dictionary, Second College Edition – Page 492
[2] Strong's Hebrew and Greek Dictionary G2189

Chapter 2

[1] Strong's Hebrew and Greek Dictionary H954
[2] Strong's Hebrew and Greek Dictionary H7664
[3] Strong's Hebrew and Greek Dictionary H8615
[4] Strong's Hebrew and Greek Dictionary H8245
[5] Strong's Hebrew and Greek Dictionary G 1252
[6] Webster's New World Dictionary, Second College Edition – Page 492
[7] Webster's New World Dictionary, Second College Edition – Page 1617

Chapter 3

[1] Webster's New World Dictionary, Second College Edition – Page1597
[2] Strong's Hebrew and Greek Dictionary G5479

Chapter 4

[1] Strong's Hebrew and Greek Dictionary H7965
[2] Strong's Hebrew and Greek Dictionary G954
Electronic Edition STEP Files Copyright © 1998, Parsons Technology, Inc.
[3] Strong's Hebrew and Greek Dictionary H3772
[4] Webster's New World Dictionary, Second College Edition – Page 1470 & Strong's Hebrew and Greek Dictionary G3141
[5] Strong's Hebrew and Greek Dictionary G3004

About The Author

Biography of
Michelle D. Houston

Michelle D. Houston was born in Tuskegee, Alabama. She is the third child out of four children born to Jewell and Helen Bell. Her parents were students at Tuskegee University where her father received his Doctorate of Veterinarian Medicine degree. Her mother, who is now retired, was an Academic Advisor at a community college in Memphis, Tennessee where they relocated and where she was reared.

After graduating from Hillcrest High School in 1981, she attended the University of Tennessee at Martin where she majored in Communications. During that time she accepted Jesus Christ as her Lord, and became actively involved in ministry there. She later received the call of God on her life to teach the uncompromised Word of God. After living in Martin for three years, she was led to relocate back to Memphis where she met Gerre Houston, her husband of 16 years. They have two children, Isaac (9), and Mikaela (4). She and her husband attended Cornerstone Theological Seminary, and Associated Christian Theological School, both located in Memphis. They presently attend and are active in ministry at Christ The Rock Metro Church where Dr. Fred and Valerie Bennett are Pastors. They are co-teachers in the Couple's Ministry; Certified Marriage specialists through the National Association of Marriage Enhancement. She is also a co-teacher of a Women's Sunday School class and the Head Photographer of Christ The Rock Metro Church.

She has been called to make a difference in the lives of God's people by being transparent, teaching them the importance of being a doer of God's Word. Her desire is to see the people of God arise, recognize and understand who they are in Christ, their purpose, their place in the home and in the body of Christ.

She is a dynamic anointed woman of faith. God has shown Himself faithful and powerful in her own life. Therefore, she gets great pleasure in seeing those who were bowed down walk upright before God, understanding who they are, and walking in the authority and victory that God has given them.

She is now at work on another book entitled *Free to be Me, by Taking Off the Mask.*

Prayer for Salvation and
Baptism in the Holy Spirit

Heavenly Father, I come to You in the Name of Jesus. Your Word says, "Whoever calls on the name of the Lord shall be saved" (Acts 2:21). I am calling on You because I desire to be saved. I believe Jesus is the Son of God Who died for me that I may live. I believe God raised Him from the dead, and is alive forever more. Therefore, Jesus I ask You to come into my heart and be Lord of my life. I receive You into my heart and now I confess You as Lord. I thank You that I am now a child of God. I am a new creation in Christ. I am saved!

Father, You also said in Your Word, "If you then, being evil, know how to give good gifts to your children, how much more will your heavenly Father give the Holy Spirit to those who ask Him!" (Luke 11:13). I am now asking You to fill me with the Holy Spirit. Holy Spirit, rise up in me as I lift up my voice in praise to God. I expect to speak with other tongues as You give me the utterance (Acts 2:4).

Begin to thank and praise God for filling you with the Holy Spirit. The words and syllables that come out of your mouth may sound strange to you because it is not in your own language, but the language given to you by the Holy Spirit.

Find a good Word church and become a part of a church family who will help you to grow in the things of God.

To contact Michelle D. Houston
write:

Michelle Houston
P.O. Box 752424
Memphis, Tennessee 38175

Email: LivingExpectantly@cfaith.com